"In *Come With Me*, Suzanne Eller opens her heart to us, wrapping poignant examples from her own life around the biblical stories of the twelve disciples. Each chapter is a compelling invitation to follow Christ in much the same way these men did, putting aside the old and embracing the new. Heartache and hardship are addressed head on, and so are the joy-filled benefits of saying yes. As the author reminds us, 'Following Jesus isn't a charmed life; it's a changed life.'"

Liz Curtis Higgs, bestselling author of *Bad Girls of the Bible*

"We love to be invited. We want to be included. We long for more. Only Jesus can truly offer all of that to us—and he does. Suzie's encouragement and insights give us what we need to say the most life-changing, soul-freeing yes our hearts will ever utter."

Holley Gerth, *Wall Street Journal* bestselling author of *You're Already Amazing*

"Every once in a while, God brings along a book you desperately need. Suzie Eller's *Come With Me* brought a clarity and focus I've prayed for, reminding me that I don't have to have all the answers . . . that I don't need to figure out which way to go. My only job is to follow Jesus. He'll take care of the rest."

Joanna Weaver, author of *Having a Mary Heart in a Martha World*

"No matter your age or stage in life, when Jesus calls you as his thirteenth disciple, you have two options: run and hide, or pick up your nets and follow. Take it deeper with the discussion questions—great for small group or personal study!"

Christine Abraham, founder and ministry director of WomensBibleCafe.com

"*Come with Me* is more than just another great read. It is an invitation to transformation. Suzie's book fanned my faith to life. It made me hungry for the Word, desperate for a fresh encounter with my Savior, and grateful for the gift of his presence. It will change the way you follow Jesus!"

Alicia Bruxvoort, Proverbs 31 Ministries writer

"Suzie's realness and vulnerability about how much her faith grew when she decided to deeply follow Jesus in a new way is a shining example of how life-changing committed faith can be. Life-changing for us as disciples, but also life-changing for those we come in contact with along the way. This is an invaluable read for anyone who longs not only to know the Father, but to follow him wherever he leads, no questions asked."

Tracie Miles, Proverbs 31 Ministries speaker and writer; author of *Your Life Still Counts*

"Suzie pushes her readers to venture out, even into the deepest waters, to follow after Jesus. This intimate look at the Lord's disciples, woven together with personal experiences, gives an intricate picture of what a life led by him can be. Her story is rich, full of life and grace."

Krista Williams, Proverbs 31 Ministries First 5 writer

Come With Me

Come With Me

Discovering *the* Beauty *of* Following Where He Leads

Suzanne Eller

BETHANYHOUSE

a division of Baker Publishing Group
Minneapolis, Minnesota

Published by Bethany House Publishers
11400 Hampshire Avenue South
Bloomington, Minnesota 55438
www.bethanyhouse.com

Bethany House Publishers is a division of
Baker Publishing Group, Grand Rapids, Michigan

Printed in the United States of America

ISBN 978-0-7642-1812-5

Library of Congress Control Number: 2016930569

Unless otherwise indicated, Scripture quotations are from the Holy Bible, New International Version®. NIV®. Copyright © 1973, 1978, 1984, 2011 by Biblica, Inc.™ Used by permission of Zondervan. All rights reserved worldwide. www.zondervan.com

Scripture quotations identified NASB are from the New American Standard Bible®, copyright © 1960, 1962, 1963, 1968, 1971, 1972, 1973, 1975, 1977, 1995 by The Lockman Foundation. Used by permission. (www.Lockman.org)

Scripture quotations identified NKJV are from the New King James Version®. Copyright © 1982 by Thomas Nelson, Inc. Used by permission. All rights reserved.

Scripture quotations identified NLT are from the *Holy Bible*, New Living Translation, copyright © 1996, 2004, 2015 by Tyndale House Foundation. Used by permission of Tyndale House Publishers, Inc., Carol Stream, Illinois 60188. All rights reserved.

Scripture quotations identified THE MESSAGE are from THE MESSAGE. Copyright © by Eugene H. Peterson 1993, 1994, 1995, 1996, 2000, 2001, 2002. Used by permission of NavPress. All rights reserved. Represented by Tyndale House Publishers, Inc.

Cover design by Brand Navigation
Cover photography by Petar Paunchev

Author is represented by The FEDD Agency, Inc.

16 17 18 19 20 21 22   7 6 5 4 3 2 1

Dedicated to Kate
Heaven just became sweeter because of you
Gaga

Contents

Acknowledgments

During the writing of this book, my husband, Richard, was diagnosed with cancer. There's nothing like deciding to pen words about walking with Jesus only to discover that you're going to have to live them with gusto. Thank you to the people who wrapped around us during that time. Some of you showed up at the hospital at 5:00 a.m. to sit with me while my husband was in surgery. Others brought food every night for nearly a month. While I fully blame you for the ten pounds I gained (who can turn down key lime pie and peanut butter cookies?), I also thank you for loving us with casserole dishes, soup, and tangible hands-on love.

To my guy who is kicking cancer like a champ, I love you like crazy. Now that we've done this cancer thing twice, I know one thing: You and I are a good team. You've championed me for the past fifteen years as I've walked this path called ministry. I love you, Richard. You are my soul mate and the man who makes me laugh like no one else.

Thank you to my children, Leslie and Stephen, Ryan and Kristin, Melissa and Josh. You pulled close around your dad and me as we made difficult decisions. Thank you for that hilarious moment in the waiting room where we laughed until we cried. No one else got it, but we did.

To my beautiful grandbabies, Elle, Luke, Jane, Audrey, Josiah, and Caleb. You make my heart full. Your love for Gaga is pure and joyful and messy and chaotic. Having six grandbabies under the age of five is a delightful whirlwind. Thank you for reminding me that deadlines are important, but those I call family are treasures.

Thank you to Kim Bangs and the Bethany team. Kim, you're my friend as well as my editor. I love how much you love Jesus and how you stand side-by-side with your authors. Thank you to the entire Bethany team, who is as much a part of this book as I am. Your creativity and heart for the project blew me away.

Thank you to Esther Fedorkevich and her team at the Fedd Agency. The day you became my literary agent was a good day. I love your honesty and your heart.

To my "Aaron," Crystal Hornback, thank you for being there when I surrendered to the truth that we all need someone, and you have been that someone times ten.

To Michele Cushatt, who wrote the foreword in the midst of healing from surgery. Your yes in the midst of a hard place rocked my world.

To the 185-plus brave #livefree girls, who are ministry partners of the best kind, thank you for everything you do and for who you are. Thank you to Tara, Jana, Pam, Christy, Carla, Christina, Crystal, Kathy, Michelle, Sarah Anne, and Heather for coming alongside as I wrote this book. Thank you for allowing me to throw chapters your way for your beautiful insight and honesty.

Thank you to my sisters at Proverbs 31 Ministries, a ministry team who reaches far beyond numbers or a spotlight to come alongside a woman seeking Jesus with all of her heart.

Last and most significant, thank you to my Savior for choosing a once-broken girl to share you with the world. I'm humbled.

Foreword

It matters little that I was only seven years old. I'll never forget it.

My mom and dad stood at my side, singing a hymn. Clearly unruffled by what I was about to do. I, on the other hand, couldn't get my stomach to stop its flip-flops. With my best puppy-pleading eyes, I asked my dad to help me do this thing. I wanted him to hold my hand, walk me down the long church sanctuary aisle, get me to the front.

But as much as I wanted him to come with me, I somehow knew he wouldn't. *Couldn't.* The decision—the journey—was mine.

In spite of my fear, in spite of the impulse to shrink from the moment and find a safe corner in which to hide, I loosed myself of my pew. Desire pulled me forward. I knew I wanted what waited for me.

Jesus!

That Sunday was to be my public declaration of devotion. My chance to let preacher, parents, and a room full of congregants know that I chose to follow Jesus. I was ready, as certain as a seven-year-old can be. Even so, the decision felt heavy on small shoulders. Now, with so many years between us, I wonder if the girl suspected the complicated life that would follow.

Nearly four decades have passed since October 29, 1978. Thirty-seven years since a simple, ordinary Sunday changed my course. In that span of time I graduated from high school and college, embarked on a few various careers, married, and raised children (*six* of them).

But I've also wrestled with divorce and single-mothering. Remarriage and stepparenting. The too-soon death of my dad. Adolescence and graduation times three. The addition of three small children and a second round of parenting.

Not to mention cancer. Three times.

Intermingled with the joys, I've wrestled with hardships far more painful than my younger self could've imagined. Countless times I've ached for an easier life, a less complicated life. Looking back on innocence, the girl so determined to break free of her pew and follow the One she loved, I can't help but think how many times, as a grown woman, I've tried to glue myself right back to it.

You see, it's one thing to sit in church talking about Jesus. It's another thing to stand up and follow him. Wherever the following leads.

Because sometimes following Jesus means trusting his redemption when your dream of marriage disappears.

Sometimes following Jesus means releasing control when a child struggles.

Sometimes following Jesus means relinquishing comfort to obey his calling.

Sometimes following Jesus means loving and forgiving when a relationship is hard.

And sometimes following Jesus means trusting his sovereignty when death knocks at your door.

I won't lie to you. At times following Jesus feels risky, costly, and hard. I've known seasons when I would've preferred to play church, keep Jesus at a distance, make my own way. It's far easier to wax poetic about faith than to grab Jesus' hand and plunge into the deep unknown with him.

Yet in spite of the struggle—perhaps because of it—I've learned that following Jesus is the only way to truly live.

Because it was Jesus who rescued and rebuilt me when divorce shattered my heart into a thousand pieces.

It was Jesus who whispered wisdom during those lonely years of parenting.

It was Jesus who taught me—teaches me still—how to relinquish control and trust his work in my husband, in my marriage, *in me*.

And it is Jesus who comes near with his peace and the promise of heaven every time terror strikes in the name of cancer.

This is what I know to be true: Suffering and hardship will come, regardless of the depth of our faith. But a shallow faith offers very little in the way of peace and comfort.

In this world you will have trouble!

Jesus guaranteed it. But he didn't stop there. He also promised himself as the salve for our suffering.

But take heart! I have overcome the world.

Here sits our choice. The same choice twelve disciples faced when he called them from their ordinary lives into risky, often hard, extraordinary ones.

Keep Jesus at a distance? Observe his work and words from afar?

Or leave the safety of our seats to follow him?

This is Suzie's invitation, one she has embraced and lived out with great passion and sincerity. Move close! Lean in! Allow your One and Only to ignite and burn to hot life the kind of faith that can withstand whatever may come.

True, it's not without cost, nor without risk. But it's also not without reward. Wisdom for the questions. Presence in the pain. Peace in the dark. And joy, no matter what comes.

Jesus awaits, my friend. Loose yourself of your pew. And run to him. *Run!*

Your life—the life you long for—depends on it.

Michele Cushatt, author, *Undone: A Story of Making Peace With an Unexpected Life*

Introduction

What would you say if Jesus walked up to you today and said these words?

Come with me.

Wherever I lead.

Whatever the price.

Do you say yes?

Imagine that your yes moves you from faith as usual to faith that changes every aspect of who you are, including how you live, the choices you make, how you think, and even how you approach life. Imagine a faith that spills out into your relationships and impacts the world, especially those within your reach.

Is that the kind of faith you want?

This is the faith that comes from saying *yes* to Jesus' invitation.

But consider this. Saying yes might lead you out of what is safe and predictable. As a grace girl, I love nothing more than the beautiful parts of my faith—like mercy, unconditional love, and the reality of his presence inside of me. But if we are honest, there are places where Jesus might lead where we don't want to linger. Like loving the unlovable, or believing for a miracle when the answer is nowhere in sight, or leaving what makes us feel comfortable to partner with God in his plan rather than our own.

Saying yes draws us to experience every aspect of our faith. That is the secret nestled in this invitation from Jesus: Every part of our faith is impactful—the welcoming places, the comforting places, and the more challenging places where we move from our will to his.

Come With Me was born after a late-night ~~wrestling match~~ conversation with my heavenly Father. I longed to experience him in greater measure. I didn't want comfortable faith, though I found comfort in my faith. I didn't want to reach the end of my life and say that the ultimate achievement of the cross was that I was "good," though I wanted his goodness in me. That night I took a sticky note and wrote the words "walk into the deep" and placed it in my Bible.

Oh, how I longed to go deeper even if that meant my faith might resemble anything but the norm.

Martin Luther once said, "First I shake the whole apple tree that the ripest might fall. Then I climb the tree and shake each limb, and then each branch and then each twig, and then I look under each leaf."

Luther looked beyond the obvious, which is where I went as well. I opened my Bible to the book of Luke and began to take up residence with the disciples. That often led me to the other gospels, shaking the limbs and twigs of the stories to see what might fall from the disciples' lives.

They became real. More than a great story. More than a lesson. These men had no idea where following Jesus would lead them. As I studied and read, I listened as they slammed into doubt. I stood in the crowd as animosity curled around them like blue-tinged flames. I wept as they listened to a blind man's cry for help and witnessed the miracle that followed.

I cringed as Jesus rebuked them, for none of us desires to be called out in our weakness or out-and-out disobedience. Yet I celebrated when they realized that he saw something inside of them that they could not see at all. These were real people with real emotions and misgivings, making hard decisions as they followed Jesus.

They didn't have the rest of the story that we have at our fingertips.

"Drop your nets" sounds exhilarating, unless you're the one saying good-bye to your dad, who's standing with his jaw open in disbelief.

"Your name is now Peter" is lovely to hear, unless it means that you are expected to be a rock that can be depended upon, and you're not exactly known for that quality.

"You feed them" is an exciting proposal, unless you're the one holding the meager lunch and see no answer in sight.

In these pivotal moments they stepped from being observers into a partnership with Jesus.

Is that same teaching for us? Every word he spoke to his disciples was spoken with the understanding that generations would hear the same words and be changed by them. Rick Warren was once asked to name the best translation of the Bible. He said, "When you translate it into your life."[1]

When we answer the call of "Come with me," something changes. It's no longer about church, though we love our church family. It's no longer about being moral just for morality's sake. It's discovering what it means for faith to infiltrate every detail of your life.

As I lingered with the disciples for several months, I realized that all believers are called to walk as the thirteenth disciple.

We can sit in the crowd. We can follow where he leads. We can listen for his voice and look for him in the ordinary.

I journaled almost daily during those months. There were many times that my words reflected a true struggle. Like the early disciples, I wasn't always certain how to respond or what to do, but I longed to at least hear what was being spoken. Throughout this book I share some of those private entries, for my prayer is that you'll journal as well. Looking back allows us to see the imprint of where we began.

As we follow Jesus as a disciple in our modern world, it shifts the dynamic from religious to relating to Jesus one-to-one; from rote prayers to exploring what it means to believe; from following expectations to responding from the heart.

How did this close relationship with Jesus impact those early followers?

It launched them into the lives of others in ways they never imagined. It caused them to act and react in a manner that didn't make sense in light of who they once were, or even how they felt. They found their part in an overall heavenly plan and were set free to run after that with abandon.

Philippians 3:8 reads, "Yes, everything else is worthless when compared with the infinite value of knowing Christ Jesus my Lord" (NLT).

Their worldview changed as it wrapped around the infinite value of knowing Jesus. Halfway into my yearlong journey, I realized how seeing myself as a disciple had changed me. One day I was at a crossroads. A decision needed to be made, and I sensed the direction that Jesus was leading. Before, I would have prayed. I might have weighed the pros and cons. In some instances, I might have sought trusted counsel. All of these are good things to do, but to be honest, sometimes I used them to delay my yes to Jesus.

This time, I imagined Simon, the tired fisherman who had no idea what Jesus was trying to offer him. I could almost hear Jesus' words:

Will you push out deeper?

I reached for my Savior's hand, knowing that if he asked, it was my privilege to say yes.

"Come with me" is an invitation that will delightfully change you forever, whether you've been a believer for years and years or you are hearing his voice for the very first time.

Will you walk it with me?

1

But If You Say So

Great people do not do great things; God does great
things through surrendered people.

Jennie Allen, *Restless: Because You Were Made for More*

If I could choose one word to describe the feeling that led me
to live this book, it would be *hungry*.

Hungry for deeper faith. Hungry for a relationship with God
that changes how I view the world around me. Hungry for his
presence to be so big on the inside of me that it shows up in
my home, my marriage, my interaction with others. Hungry
for more than the status quo, even if that means I need to be
brave. One of my favorite songs, "Ocean," describes what I
desired from this journey, which is to "trust without borders."
It didn't take long to realize that singing these words and living
them are very different.

Come Sit With Simon Peter

My husband used to work rotating night shifts. There's a phrase passed around the mill for guys who work there. It's the GP Shuffle—the way a guy walks after years of working at the mill, his shins and feet aching from wearing steel-toed boots on concrete for twelve hours at a stretch. That's who I thought about as I sat close to Simon Peter.

He's fished all night long with no success. A weary Simon, James, and John wash their heavy fishing nets while not far away a large crowd surrounds Jesus of Nazareth, the man everyone has been talking about. The fishermen wash their nets, their bodies aching for sleep. When they complete their task, Simon returns to his boat only to find Jesus sitting inside.

"Push me out in deeper water," Jesus says.

The worn, weather-beaten, fishy-smelling vessel is a perfect floating platform. The crowd can't see or hear Jesus well on the shore, but if he stands in the boat, they'll see him perfectly. Simon grabs hold of the fishing boat and pushes from shore. Later, when the crowd disperses, Jesus has another request for fatigued Simon: "Now go out where it is deeper, and let down your nets to catch some fish" (Luke 5:4 NLT).

Have you ever had someone ask you to do something that makes no sense in the natural?

What do you do if that request comes from Jesus? Maybe you wrestle with it. I know I have. So does Simon. This isn't an easy request. The fishing nets of that day are circular and weighted around the perimeter with rocks and other heavy materials. It's the most prized tool of a fisherman other than his boat, and washing is imperative to maintain them.

Fishing again means washing the nets again. Then there's the reality that the fish aren't swimming into the nets. Jesus remains steadfast in his request, and that places Simon clearly at a crossroad. He doesn't *have* to push out the boat. Simon Peter is the boss of his own life. He can turn around and call it a day if he wishes.

He doesn't. Instead he replies, "But if you say so, I'll let the nets down again."

But if you say so.

Can you hear the conflict in his answer? Simon Peter is the fisherman, not Jesus. He's trawled for fish for years under his father's tutelage; it's how he makes his living. Jesus' telling him to fish one more time after an unproductive all-nighter is like the person who has never had children telling you how to discipline yours in Walmart.

Is Jesus a teacher? Yes. Is he the Savior? Simon's not quite sure about that yet. But Jesus is definitely not a fisherman. Simon knows that for a fact.

This flesh-and-blood man who is exhausted to the core does it anyway. What compels him to push into deeper waters when he doesn't feel like it? What might his answer of "But if you say so" teach those of us who desperately long to hear the voice of Jesus but who sometimes resist?

Come With Me

Don't Miss Out on Your Greatest Opportunity

Simon is not unfamiliar with this man called Jesus. In Mark 1:14–20, Simon is introduced to Jesus by his brother, Andrew. In that very first meeting Jesus called the brothers to follow him, and they did. Simon dropped his nets, just like that. He even had a name change. Jesus informed Simon that he was to be called Peter, which means "rock." There are two distinctive encounters with Jesus. The first, where Jesus asks him to drop his nets, and the second, the day that Jesus waits for Simon Peter in his boat. Biblical scholar G. Campbell Morgan writes:

> A few weeks before, certainly not more than a few weeks, He had called these men to follow, and they had left boats, nets, and fathers and mothers, kith and kin, and had gone. Now we have no details, but we have the fact, that they were back at the business again.[1]

Simon dropped his nets and followed Jesus, but at some point he went back to fishing. Was it out of necessity? Had he dropped his nets out of curiosity, only to find his way back to his old life? We aren't told that information. Instead, the fact that Jesus is perched in a boat waiting on Simon tells us far more about our Savior than it does the fisherman.

He pursued Simon Peter, even after Simon said yes and then went back to fishing. Jesus knew exactly where to find Simon. It was no surprise to Jesus that Simon was doing the same ol', same ol'. It was no surprise to Jesus that Simon was tired, fatigued, and discouraged after fishing all night with nothing to show for it. He also knew what Simon Peter did not: There were deeper waters ahead for Simon.

Have you ever resisted his call to walk into the deep? I have. We hear Jesus calling us to go deeper or to trust or to believe that he knows what we do not, and we start to explain all the reasons that it just doesn't make sense. How many times have I battled what God is speaking into my heart, when he's trying to give me my greatest opportunity?

To trust him. To experience more than the same ol', same ol' in my faith. To actually believe that he's Lord in my life and that he's in the boat with me. When I resist or walk away, have I missed his plan entirely? Not so!

Let's watch as Jesus asks Simon to cast his nets. He lets them down, and suddenly the nets fill, nearly toppling the boat with the weight of scrambling fish. He frantically shouts out to James and John to bring their boat over. More fish fill the nets, and both boats are on the verge of sinking. In the midst of this miracle Simon falls to his knees. "Oh, Lord, please leave me—I'm too much of a sinner to be around you (Luke 5:8 NLT)."

What we hear is not terror, but awe. He's just rediscovered this man called Jesus. Just think, he almost chose the familiar and comfortable over his greatest opportunity.

When I refuse to go deeper, my faith lingers in the shallow.

How many times do I choose to sit in the shallow end when Jesus longs to take me deeper? How many times have I felt God asking me to do something that makes no sense to me, and I argue with him? Too often I've pointed out the impossibilities or obstacles, as if he's not God and doesn't see further down the road. I have requested assurance that it's all going to work out just like I think it should, and *then* I'll push out deeper. I may even hold up an accounting of all the times I tried and it failed, because I've somehow come to believe that faith equals success every time—failing to understand that he's calling me not to success but to faith in him.

Sometimes I start to follow, and then I turn around and climb back into the comfortable places where I'm not challenged and I'll never change. It's the last place I really want to be, but it takes too much faith to do anything different.

Simon Peter became the rock. He saw lame men leap to their feet, healed! He walked on water, if only for a few seconds. Crowds lingered in the streets, hoping that his shadow might fall upon them and heal them (Acts 5:15). Though we know these things, Simon didn't as he threw out his nets.

It was only as he sailed into territory that sometimes felt way over his head or experienced forgiveness and grace as he walked with Jesus or climbed the harder paths of faith that he became the rock that Jesus knew he could be.

If Simon hadn't dropped his nets a second time, what words would describe his story? Perhaps his life would have been described as safe. Familiar. A man with salt on his cheeks as he fished all night.

A fisher of men? I don't think so.

"Push Out Deeper" Is Your Invitation

My husband worked at the factory job for nearly two decades, and a part of him—the vibrant part that drew me to him in the beginning—was fading. I encouraged him to move from this job that paid well but robbed him of his personality and energy. When he didn't, I grew impatient.

Then there were the moments when I was just sad.

There were physical implications to standing on concrete for twelve hours at a time, but the shift work messed with his well-being. This was the change most evident after years of working in the plant. My gregarious husband fell into silence. His theory was that if he opened his mouth, the way he felt inside might escape and affect his family. I wanted to fix him. I wanted to make him leave his job because I was ready for it. I wanted to entice him with smiles and silliness to make him laugh again when he felt like doing anything but. One night I lay in bed while tears ran down my face. I loved this guy with everything I had in me and I wasn't going anywhere, but I missed the man I married.

I don't know why nighttime is when God and I meet most often; perhaps it's the only time he has my total attention. But Jesus walked into my sadness. I felt him asking me to believe that fixing or manipulating or twirling away in all of my own efforts wasn't the answer, and that there was a plan for Richard.

More so, that plan might not look like mine. It might not take place at the rate I thought it should.

Was I willing to trust?

Yes and no. There's a hushed and holy place inside of believers where we instinctively understand that God is leading us in one direction or another, but not far away are the emotions that shout, "Just fix it. Don't make me push out in deeper water. Make this easy for me. Do it, God!"

Which do I choose?

I placed my hands over my husband's sleeping body as tears soaked my pillow.

I'm willing to believe.

I didn't know that Richard would leave the factory job months later. I had no idea that we'd sell our home and almost everything we owned to pay tuition as he finished his bachelor's and master's degrees and completed clinical supervisory hours to become a licensed therapist. I didn't know that the man I married would return to me and that his funky dance moves would entice me to laugh—and that I would happily join in.

This is often the hardest part of trusting Jesus.

There's no blueprint. There's no peek at the final product. Simon Peter couldn't see the end result. Instead he was asked to live moment by moment and day by day, walking with Jesus. The "rock" was honed and carved each time he whispered the words "But if you say so." We are changed in the same manner. It's not an it-all-works-out-in-the-end guarantee, but an experience of relationship and trust. We listen, and if it's God's voice, we respond even when we're not sure of the outcome.

A year after Richard left his job, his body adjusted to normal hours and unrestricted sleep. Vibrant color returned to his personality. He started running. First a mile, then two, and eventually five or six miles each time. This is where I started to see all the pieces falling into place. My guy was his old self. Our marriage became a source of joy once again—normal, but normal was beautiful. Richard moved from an internship at a drug and alcohol center to an official position in a counseling agency.

We had pushed out in deeper waters and it all worked out.

Except . . . Jesus didn't stop asking us to push out into deeper waters. In my life, there was a second time and a third, then more after that, and they keep coming. Not all of our deeper-water experiences can be tied in tidy testimonials. I'll share more of my own stories that took place even as I wrote this book, some of the hardest that I've walked through. I promise that there were times my words were not an immediate yes. Instead, I whispered, "But if you say so."

Our encounters with Jesus as his disciple become less about the end destination and more about the invitation to trust

I trust that You have a plan for good, and not for harm (Jeremiah 29:11). I trust that if you say go, and even though I want to hold up a fistful of excuses and objections, that going is exactly where I should be.
<u>But if you say so, Lord.</u>

him, wherever that leads, whatever he asks us to do. For Jesus meets us where we are with one plan in mind: to change us forever.

I don't know what your "boat" is, but he plunks down right in the center of it. He sits in the midst of a hurting marriage and asks us to love when we really want to walk away. He takes a seat in our uncertainties and asks us to believe he can use our lives for his good. He waits in our parenting pain and asks us to hold on to the promise whispered the day that child was born. He walks into our finances and asks us to give when we really want to hold on. He settles into our anxiousness when we've been waiting for longer than we hoped.

Whisper yes where no wants to take root.

So how do we respond?

Accept the invitation. It's okay to acknowledge your doubts, for that's what you do in any healthy relationship—you're honest when you're not sure how it's all going to work out. But this is where change takes place.

Say yes where no wants to take root.

It's Not About the Fish

Can you imagine the joy Simon experiences at the catch of fish? It's a miracle! It will provide for his family. Simon could build a shrine dedicated to the miracle and profit from it. At the very least, he might set up a fishing clinic and show others how to catch a lot of fish too.

Simon walked away from the fish to follow Jesus (Luke 5:11). That changes the perspective entirely. The miracle was never about the fish. Pushing out deeper was never about the fish. That voice asking you to push out deeper? It's not about the *fish*. Simon walked away from a heap of fish and Jesus became . . .

Healer
Savior
Forgiver
Provider
Lord

That's the real miracle performed in Simon Peter's life, and it's what we discover as his disciples when we say yes—just because he asks. We open our heart to the miracle of walking with Jesus. Maybe he's asking you to trust, and your thoughts go something like this:

- What will I lose (or gain) if I say yes?
- Will I fall flat on my face? If I do, what will people think?
- Am I equipped for this?
- This is not happening on my timetable, so I'll just do this my way.

The focus is the fish, or lack thereof. What if you changed the question to "What miracle is Jesus trying to perform in me?"

If you're a planner, the thought of saying yes when you don't have all the answers might be frightening. This isn't a call to blindly thrust out on your own, but rather to listen closely to the Holy Spirit that lives within you and to take the next step.

Simon Peter would never have caught the fish in his net if he had not sailed to the middle of the lake and thrown out his nets. Jesus didn't throw up a PowerPoint to detail the entire map of Simon's life. Thank goodness, for most of us would tremble at the thought of walking in Simon Peter's shoes. He simply asked him to take the next step.

Let's go fishing, Simon.

Jesus never promised Simon or any of his disciples that following him was a one-time, no-risk-involved, feel-safe-and-comfortable-always venture. In fact, he often assured them of the opposite.

We are asked to push out deeper a second, third, fourth time.

What is God asking you to do? Have you resisted? Has the focus been on the results or on the obstacles over the joy of walking with Jesus?

If so, let's whisper it together.

But if you say so.

Taking It Deeper

1. Read Luke 5:1–7. In what way do you sense Jesus calling you to push the boat out into deeper waters?

2. What might one small step look like for you?

3. "It's not about the fish." Describe your response to that statement.

4. What has been your focus (your fish)? Share one way you sense God asking you to shift that focus.

5. Read Luke 5:8–11. Perhaps you had a parent say, "Because I said so," and that offers a negative connotation. How is this call to trust in Jesus different?

6. Simon was awestruck by Jesus. Are you? Invite the Holy Spirit (read Psalm 51:12) to ignite that awe within you once again. (Make that a prayer and share it here.)

7. What does it mean to whisper yes where no wants to take root?

SCRIPTURE

When he had finished speaking, he said to Simon, "Now go out where it is deeper, and let down your nets to catch some fish."

"Master," Simon replied, "we worked hard all last night and didn't catch a thing. But if you say so, I'll let the nets down again."

Luke 5:4–5 NLT

PRAYER

Lord, if you ask, that's enough for me. I will follow you. I'll take a step into deeper waters and walk with you. I offer up my fears and climb in the boat, for you are with me.

LIVING AS A DISCIPLE

- If you sense his leading, whisper yes where no wants to take root.
- Give greater weight to walking with Jesus over the end results.
- Take one small step and celebrate your new journey of faith.

2

You Don't Mean Me, Do You?

Christianity, when it's all said and done, is about following Jesus Christ and becoming every day more and
more like him.

Bob Hostetler, *The Red Letter Life*

I remember the first time that confidence felt . . . *right*.

People became just people. An unfamiliar situation wasn't
overwhelming but exciting. Rather than worry about my words
or about doing something that could potentially be embarrass-
ing, I learned to laugh at how awkward we all can be at times.
It was light-years from the insecure girl I once was.

The thing is, Jesus didn't wait until I felt confident to invite
me to walk with him or to do works in his name. My first

attempts in ministry might make me cringe if I took the time to think about them, but I don't because those fumbling attempts were my training ground. It's where I grew through mistakes. It's where I discovered the power of offering grace to myself and starting again. Sure, some human beings seem to brim with quiet self-assurance from the womb, but most of us ease into it with wisdom that is hard earned. Now that I'm in my fifties (seriously, how did that happen so fast?), I've finally embraced the truth that we never officially "arrive."

Where we go is not nearly as important as who we go with.

We'll never know all that Jesus can teach us. We'll never tap so deep into the power of the Holy Spirit that we deplete it. We can never announce that we've done all that God wants to do through us and we're done—kaput. We are continually becoming the parent, the person, the believer, the warrior, the difference-maker that resides inside.

I sat in an arena a couple of years ago watching a tiny woman standing on the large stage under bright lights. She held up a black bag. "Some of you may have seen this craft before. I show it a lot because it's the only craft I've ever completed. I asked God to give me a visual aid. Something that would show you how I feel sometimes."

With perfect timing Patsy Clairmont pulled out a wad of colorful yarn, blues and reds and yellows, all knotted and tangled and a mess. The audience erupted in laughter. It was the perfect visual. As I listened to her speak, I wondered if she'd done this for years. When I read her book *I Grew Up Little*, I was surprised to discover she had not. There had been a time she couldn't get out of bed, much less stand on a stage in front of thousands. She says:

I was lost in an emotional thundercloud; I was blind to any path that might lead me out of my despair; I was mentally muddled, and my faltering walk was one of obvious dysfunction. [1]

That dysfunction kept her in bed on most days. One day she felt God asking her to make her bed. That might not seem like a big request—unless your bed has been your hiding place. Patsy describes tucking the corners in and smoothing the blanket and symbolically beginning a new path toward healing.

Do you relate to the apprehension that rises when God asks you to do something and you feel ill-equipped? Maybe it's parenting when you haven't had a great example. Or believing for a strong marriage when all you've seen is divorce or conflict. It can be as simple as looking someone in the eye and realizing that you have something to offer in the conversation.

Maybe you've had people say that you are not the right person for the job. In most cases, it's our own thoughts that are the biggest battlefield. We point to someone else.

Choose her, God. I think she can do it.

Yet he chooses you. He chooses me. He chooses each of us, if we are willing.

Let's Have Dinner With Matthew

Jesus is in a lonely place praying all night (Luke 6:12). The stakes are high. Not far away a crowd is sleeping. Among that growing multitude are the curious, the converted, and those desperate to be healed. It also includes men who condemn what Jesus is doing. The Pharisees and teachers of the religious law are never very far away (Luke 5:17).

Jesus is praying all night because he plans to choose twelve men the next morning as his apostles (Luke 4:18–19). Whoever is chosen will travel from village to village, sometimes with only a rock upon which to lay their head at night. They will leave family and homes and businesses behind. It's a path of suffering and hardship cobbled with joy and deep discovery. Those chosen will build a kingdom that will outlive them to impact generations. They will also be mocked. They will be misunderstood and their good names maligned. They will be placed higher in esteem than perhaps their character is ready to withstand.

Though we are not privy to his prayer, I've spent time in leadership meetings where thoughtful men and women made hard decisions as they chose a team. I wonder if Jesus' conversation with God went something like this:

God: What about Simon Peter?

Jesus: He's one of the older guys, but he's a little impetuous.

God: Have you considered the brothers, James and John?

Jesus: Sometimes the brothers have their own best interests at heart.

God: What about Matthew?

Jesus: Wow, Matthew . . . I'm not sure anyone will understand that choice.

After seeking God all night long, at daybreak Jesus calls out the names. Simon (whom he named Peter), Andrew, James, John, Philip, Bartholomew, Matthew, Thomas, James (son of Alphaeus), Simon (who was called the Zealot), Judas (son of James), and Judas Iscariot. Some of these men are obvious choices.

Matthew the tax collector is not.

In Jesus' day, tax collectors wielded power over their neighbors and kinsman. The tax system was corrupt. Jews were taxed by the government heavily. Chief tax collectors employed publicans to help them gather that money. The publicans were paid through an inflated "fee" that never made it to the coffers of the government, and authorities turned a blind eye to the injustice. The Jews paid government taxes, local taxes, and temple taxes. It was a heavy burden, and many feared the men who counted their crops and demanded payment—especially those who did so using fear tactics.

On the day that Jesus passed the toll station by the sea, simply asking a tax collector to follow him was scandalous. When Jesus asked Matthew to be one of the Twelve, it was unimaginable.

Yet from the moment that Jesus met Matthew, he looked beyond his job title to see the man. Matthew was a Levite. Generations of his people had been marked as men of God. Somewhere along the way, Matthew got lost. It wasn't inconceivable that his family hung their heads in shame when their son's name was mentioned.

Matthew's choice wasn't without benefits. Power. Money. Authority. It also wasn't without a high price tag. He had lost his true identity.

Very few of us see ourselves the way God does. For too many years I saw myself as a girl raised in brokenness who had little to offer, even after I became a woman. God called me away from that identity. He saw me differently. He saw a woman who loved him. He saw a woman who desired to be a good mom. He saw things inside of me that I couldn't envision.

I don't know how you view yourself, or if the thought of being handpicked by God to follow him delights you or makes you want to hide under the bed, but Jesus called Matthew so that he could come *home*.

Home isn't a place, but a connection with Christ to the point that we know whose we are. It also allows us to see others as he does.

41

When you accept that call, you begin the process of leaving.

Patsy left her bed.

Matthew left a corrupt lifestyle of power and money.

I left insecurity.

What is he asking you to leave?

Come With Me

Where Is He Taking Us?

When Matthew embraced the truth that Jesus chose him, that led to other choices. He was one of the few who could use a pen, so he became the first to record Jesus' teachings. Those recordings became the book of Matthew. The skills that qualified him to serve as a tax collector were now in the service of Jesus.

Who knew?

Jesus did.

A few years ago I received a call to speak at a church in Fayetteville, Arkansas. A ministry called Potter's House planned an overnight retreat for eight women. I've had the privilege of speaking to large crowds, but this small conference of eight will always be my favorite. In the beginning the women were cautious. They didn't know me. But as the weekend unfolded, we prayed together, studied God's Word together, and wept together. His presence was strong in that small hotel room. When the conference ended, I climbed in my Prius and drove the winding roads through Northwest Arkansas back to Oklahoma. Tears flowed. Similar to Paul's experience in Acts 16:9, I knew that life was about to take a U-turn. I didn't have details. I didn't have a timeline. All I knew was that it had something to do with those women, and things were about to change.

When I arrived home, I stumbled into the house saying something profound like, "Umm, I think we are supposed to move to Arkansas." To his credit, Richard didn't remind me of the past five years of schooling or the thousands of hours of licensing he had just completed to become a licensed counselor. He didn't remind me that we'd been in the same church for thirty years. He didn't list all the reasons that this was a crazy idea.

He promised to pray about it.

A few weeks passed and we went back to visit the church in Fayetteville. The service ended and we walked to our car. I looked over at Richard and saw that his face was wet with tears.

"We're moving, aren't we?" I said.

This is where it gets complicated. Perhaps you are not hesitant at all about being chosen. You want to be exactly where God leads you. You're signed up, ready to go, hands waving in the air. *Pick me. Pick me. Pick me!* Whether it's a move, a ministry position, a dream, a relationship, a calling, or something within your family—you're ready for it. You are in launch mode. And then it takes longer than you think, or it appears that it will never happen.

I mentally moved to Northwest Arkansas long before we arrived. Transferring Richard's counseling license was the first hurdle, due to differing requirements of each state. He had to study for and retake the licensing exam for our new state. Each state calculated supervisory hours differently. Every time we thought we were close to the finish line, a letter arrived in the mail outlining one more class, a few more hours of supervision, one more exam. One year passed, and then another.

When we finally received the important piece of paper that said he was licensed in both Oklahoma and Arkansas, I excitedly put our house up for sale. I watched reruns on HGTV and painted and stripped all the personal items from the walls. We priced it competitively. I staged it and took pictures. We called a Realtor and started looking for new homes in Arkansas.

Only to begin a second wait. Our home didn't sell. One month. Two months. We dropped the price. Three months. Four months. We dropped the price again, lower than the purchase price six years earlier. Sometimes I'd sit on the couch with scratched-up totals running in columns on a piece of paper. The price of the house minus closing costs, minus painting, minus the real estate fee. It added up significantly. To add to our challenge, we lived in a slow market but were moving to a thriving market. On weekends we'd hand a list of ten houses to the Realtor in our new state, and five would be under contract before we made it to their door.

Only to return to our home to wait for the offer that never came.

Richard found a counseling job and moved to Arkansas while I remained home to sell the house. We lived separately for months.

Can we just be honest? It's murky when you know you've heard Jesus whisper, "I've chosen you for this," and then it doesn't work out like you think it should or the timing isn't what you hoped it would be.

This is often where we take a detour while people quote something like, "Well, if it's God's will, then the doors would have opened."

What we learned during that season is that closed doors are not always from God. Certainly there are times that a closed door is an answer to prayer, but sometimes a closed door is just a closed door. Others times it's a direct attack of the enemy, who doesn't want you to go where Jesus is leading. There were many prayer meetings across the kitchen table as Richard and I sat and held hands.

"Are you in this, God?" we asked.

Those prayers always led us to this: We were to keep on going. If God spoke it, he meant it. Our response was to move ahead.

In our case, it appeared that we were moving to Arkansas, but he wasn't leading us just to a new job or even a ministry. He was leading us to trust. It took us nearly three years to move to Arkansas after I heard him say, "Come with me, Suz."

Those three years were not in vain. When we were praying across the table for God's direction, it wasn't an exercise in futility. It was inviting the God of the universe into our choices, our doubts, and our discouragements. It was listening and crowding out the distraction and naysaying from less-precious voices to truly tune in.

> After that He went out and noticed a tax collector named Levi sitting in the tax booth, and He said to him, "Follow Me." And he left everything behind, and got up and began to follow Him.
>
> Luke 5:27–28 NASB

Matthew left everything. As Jesus' disciple, we are asked to leave as well. It might not be a move to Arkansas (I can hear you saying, "Thank God!"), but he is asking you to trust him wherever he leads.

You leave the opinion of those who say, "She's not who I would have picked," to decide that if Jesus chooses you, that's sufficient.

Years earlier, my first act of leaving was to address my lack of confidence. It didn't happen immediately, but every time I looked into the Word of God and saw that my name was engraved on the palm of his hand, my assurance grew. Just the other day I shared with hundreds of women this beautiful promise in Hebrews 4:16:

Faith begs us to climb out of the familiar.

Let us then approach God's throne of grace with confidence, so that we may receive mercy and find grace to help us in our time of need.

These were a few of their responses.

- "I don't dare walk into his presence like that. I'm not worthy."
- "I make so many mistakes, Suzie."
- "I've been told my whole life that I am a disappointment to God."
- "How is it possible to walk in with such ease?"

I wanted to put my head in my hands and weep. But their responses reminded me of a young woman who years earlier felt Jesus call her name and willingly ran to him, but who also struggled because she had no idea that Jesus saw the woman he had created her to be. My job in that moment was to remind each of them that "God often proves Himself when we feel we have the least to offer."[2]

It's not about where you are going or what you'll be doing, or how equipped or ill-equipped you feel. Being chosen (and accepting that gift) leads to leaving, which leads you home. Not to a place or a job or a person, but into confidence that wherever you are and whatever season you are in, you are his.

Being Chosen Doesn't Make It Easy

James Hudson Taylor, an English missionary to China in the nineteenth century, said, "I have found that there are three stages in every great work of God: first, it is impossible, then it is difficult, then it is done."[3]

Well, that's exciting. Who wants to sign up for that?

You hear his voice and start to plan. That's a natural response. But when it doesn't work out like you thought it would, it can make you feel stuck or that you're a failure or that somehow you misheard. Listen, if you said yes to God and you are trusting him, you are courageous. That's faith! You are far from stuck.

You're moving. To be stagnant is to never move. It's staying away from the hard parts. It's throwing your hands up in the air and giving up. The fact that you feel stuck can be a sign that you *are* moving! Due to the work that God is doing in your heart, you are aware of those days that you aren't progressing like you want to. You hunger for all that God has for you. There was a time when you would have settled in your comfort zone, content and cozy. That's not you. If you are doing all that he has asked and the timeline isn't moving the way you think it should, you are likely in a place of growth.

> *Feeling stuck is different from being stagnant.*

Matthew's saying *yes* to Jesus to serve as an apostle was exactly where God began to work powerfully in him.

Patsy's making her bed was far from the "done" stage, but it was a pivotal moment where her life was completely altered by obedience over fear.

When I looked in the mirror and saw his handiwork, that was a new beginning.

Every part of your walk with Jesus matters.

James Hudson Taylor said there were three parts: impossible, difficult, done.

I respect that, because there are times it feels exactly like that. But we can reframe it, choosing to see it as: incredible, adventure, ongoing.

You Are Part of the Bigger Picture

We finally sold our home and found a new home in Arkansas. I never shared the full details of why we were moving with the women's ministry leader I had met three years earlier. I was certain it would come across as more than a little odd to say, "You know that retreat three years ago? Well, I think we are moving because of that."

After we moved in, I called her and asked if I could come by and see her. We sat on her back deck, and I began with the tale of my weeping most of the way home from the retreat. I told her how I knew God had asked us to move to Arkansas. I explained how every single door had shut and how we knew we were to keep going.

Then I said, "I don't really even know why I'm here."

That was the truth. It didn't hit me until the last box was unpacked. We had asked God for the answers. Detailed answers hadn't come, only the reassurance that we were to move. I knew it had something to do with the ladies at the retreat, but it took so long to get there that I never told her my story. Why tell her on the off chance that things didn't work out?

She wiped away tears as the sun blanketed us. Then she proceeded to fill in the blanks—the parts I couldn't see. After watching the connection that happened between the ladies at the retreat, she prayed out of her longing. She loved the ministry, but she was exhausted. She had been praying for a while for someone to help her. Someone who would love the ladies, and who they would love back. God, in his infinite mercy and care, chose that day to pick me.

She left the retreat with a prayer on her heart.

I left the retreat with her prayer buried in mine. Not because I was anything special. Not because there weren't others who could do this job. I believe God called my name out of his love for Lynn. He gave her a desire of her heart. Fully three years after God called us to move to Arkansas, I started serving side by side with Lynn. To this day I'm privileged to co-lead this ministry for women and meet for dinner and Bible study at my home every Wednesday.

While I am grateful that God had Lynn on his heart that day, I believe he had me in mind as well. Not too long ago I was walking with one of my friends from the Potter's House Bible study.

I had received really hard news, and I hadn't had time to process it yet. We were sweaty and tired and nearly at the end of our walk when I finally spilled what was weighing so heavy. She placed her hands on my shoulders and prayed. Right there on the trail.

Right where I needed it most, because the burden was staggering. Sure, I was chosen to leave my home church, my extended family, and my comfort zone to love these women, but in return I gained feisty, honest, raw, and beautiful friends who challenge me, love me, and keep me coming back for more of Jesus. They strip the bubble wrap off of me in a hundred different ways.

Look at her, Jesus. She's raw and somewhat broken, but so beautiful to you. Look at that one, Lord. I think she has the heart of a Bible teacher. Let me walk with my friends and show them that each is chosen by you. Not her circumstances. Not her past. Not what others think.

Thank you for choosing me for this beautiful work.

—Suzie

I never know what Bible study is going to look like, and I love that. It's often funny, full of tears, always in my face, and honest beyond words. Sometimes it's hard because I don't always have answers. I wish that some things would change for a friend, but it's beyond my ability to fix.

God didn't choose me to fix anyone; that's his job. He just asked me to show up and allow him to do his work because he loves *them*. He chooses us because there's an eternal impact on us and on others. I believe one day we'll have an eye-opening view of what God was doing when he called our names to do his work.

We Are All Chosen

After his conversion, Matthew asks Jesus to come to his home for dinner. His servants prepare a feast, and Matthew gathers his peers. While they are dining, the religious rulers stand outside and witness Jesus eating with publicans and sinners. This breaks every rule. Hospitality is a big deal. Martha Stewart has nothing on the rules of that day. Sitting at someone's table for a meal as a guest is an honor. When you are a teacher—a celebrity of sorts—and you sit at someone's table, it brings honor to the household as well. That makes these guys angry. This isn't mild frustration, but shake-your-fists, red-in-the-face, tear-your-robe rage.

> *Serving others isn't a reflection of us, but of God's working through us.*

Why would Jesus, who professed to be a holy man, eat with such scum? Yes, that's the word they use (Luke 5:30 NLT). *Scum.* They are so focused on the fact that Jesus is in the home of a tax collector that they fail to understand one exquisite truth. Matthew was lost, but now he's found! When you are the one sheep lost from the ninety-nine and Jesus purposely searches for you and chooses you (Luke 5:32; 15:4), you can't help but tell others about that miracle.

Matthew isn't hosting a party to show off his relationship with Jesus, but rather to introduce Jesus to sinners and publicans who are just as lost as he is.

This was one of those moments where I stood as the thirteenth disciple. It confused me. I shook the limbs of this story so that I might grow in the process. This is what I took away from it. Matthew was in need of rescue from his badness, but the religious leaders were in desperate need of rescue from their own goodness.

As disciples, we're not to be like the religious guys standing out in the street throwing a big fit. There's work to be done. People to pray for and a message to share. There's more to do than can ever be accomplished by one person or even one million. What might happen if we all joined in—the holy and the works-in-progress, the mature and the not-as-mature, the talented and not-as-talented—and started seeking that one lost sheep together? The kingdom would grow. That's a very churchy reference, but it's appropriate. Our kingdom would shrink and his would grow.

We can either be tight-fisted with our faith or share the treasure.

One of the most devastating blows to the Christian faith is the fact that we pull apart instead of realizing we're better together. We point out our differences, when our common ground is a belief in Jesus. We build our own little kingdoms, brick by brick, shutting people out, when the call is to bring them in. How do we recognize when our faith is becoming less about his kingdom and more about our own?

- Are we angry that a "Matthew" shines when we've been faithful longer?
- Are we tempted to point out another's badness to make our goodness shine that much brighter?
- Do we resent that another person, another church, another ministry is doing well, and think it unfair rather than celebrate their reach with the gospel?
- When someone good falls, do we judge rather than help them back up?

These are hard questions, but they are also insightful. When we ask these questions, we start to rejoice that we are all chosen and need only to choose to accept the gift. We also discover our part to play.

> We don't play the major role. If we did, we'd probably go around bragging that we'd done the whole thing! No, we neither make nor save ourselves. God does both the making and saving. He creates each of us by Christ Jesus to join him in the work he does, the good work he has gotten ready for us to do, work we had better be doing.
>
> Ephesians 2:9–10 THE MESSAGE

The religious guys wanted the major role. They missed out on sitting around the table too, watching Jesus touch the hearts of people who desperately needed saving.

TAKING IT DEEPER

1. Jesus chose twelve men. He also chooses us. Share a time when you knew he was calling your name.

2. Jesus asked the disciples to leave everything behind. Is there something God is asking you to leave behind?

3. What do you think happened within Patsy as she began to make her bed?

4. Was there a time you thought it was impossible to [fill in the blank] and yet you did it anyway? Regardless of the outcome, acknowledge how courageous that was. Put it into words.

5. Suzie said it isn't where you are going, but who you are going with. What does that mean?

6. Contrast the two crowds that gathered in Luke 5:27–32. Do we modern-day believers ever act the same way?

7. One crowd needed rescuing from their badness, and the other from their own goodness. Which crowd needed Jesus the most?

8. According to Ephesians 2:13, we were created for what reason?

SCRIPTURE

Later, as Jesus left the town, he saw a tax collector named Levi [Matthew] sitting at his tax collector's booth. "Follow me and be my disciple," Jesus said to him. So Levi got up, left everything, and followed him.

Luke 5:27–28 NLT

PRAYER

Jesus, thank you for seeing me for who I am. Lead me to reveal your love to others. You've chosen me, and I step into that gift with a willing heart.

LIVING AS A DISCIPLE

• If God is asking you to leave something behind, take one small step.
• Don't automatically consider a closed door as a no.
• Encourage another believer, especially one who feels ill-equipped.

3

The Hungry, the Fatherless, and the Heart of God

When we think full-time ministry is some sort of a higher calling, we dramatically undermine our calling and impact as followers of Jesus Christ. . . . If there is such a thing as full-time ministry, we are all in it.

Peter Greer, *The Spiritual Danger of Doing Good*

With a three-and-a-half-year-old, a two-and-a-half-year-old, and a just-turned-one-year-old, Ashley and Andrew Brill's lives were full. Yet both had a gnawing feeling that God was beginning a new push, a new *something*. They just didn't know what it was. They started to pray.

God, is there something you're asking us to do?

One day Ashley went to an informational meeting for 99 Balloons, a ministry supporting children and families with special needs. When the meeting ended, she grabbed a prayer card for a little boy named Sergei who lived in an orphanage 99 Balloons worked with overseas. Over the next few days she quickly grew attached to the little guy on the card and started praying for him daily. One night she and Andrew lay in bed and prayed for Sergei, asking God to move mountains on his behalf.

Was it possible that their family was the answer?

The next day Ashley called to see if there was a possibility of adopting him. They received recent pictures of Sergei, as well as videos a mission therapy team had taken. Five days later Ashley received a phone call from the ministry. Unfortunately, Sergei had already been adopted. Ashley was heartbroken . . . and joyful. It was exactly what she and Andrew had prayed over him. She wept in joy for Sergei but grieved over her own loss, for she had already started to fall in love with him.

Ashley felt God had led them to this particular orphanage. She definitely believed that he had moved on their hearts to adopt. Andrew wanted to know for certain that this was the right path to take for their family. Ashley was ready to go . . . now! The one thing they agreed on was that they needed to be on the same page, so they asked God to drop either yes or no in both of their hearts.

Several months passed. As they waited, Ashley prayed a prayer adapted from Psalm 25:4: "Show us the path where we should walk, O Lord; point out the right road for us to follow."

One day Andrew asked if they could talk once the children were in bed.

"I think adopting a special-needs child is what God has for us," he said, pulling her close.

For the rest of the evening they joyfully talked. Every conversation led back to the special-needs orphanage in Ukraine. When they contacted the ministry, they learned about a little girl named Paulina. She was three and a half years old and lived in the severe special-needs room of the orphanage. She couldn't see. She couldn't speak. She couldn't walk.

God saw her. He spoke on her behalf. He began to move Ashley and Andrew toward her with open arms.

Let's Get to Know James the Elder

James the Elder was one of two disciples named James and was John's older brother. He was a fisherman, but scholars believe that his family was one of the more affluent in the fishing community.

Have you ever met a person who always wants to be first? You know, those who push ahead in the line so they don't have to wait. The person who parks in the red zone because they're just going in "for a minute." James and his family seem to be those kind of people. One day James the Elder's mother approaches Jesus and gets down on her knees.

"Jesus, place my sons at the right and left side of the throne when you become King."

Most Jews believed the Messiah would arrive as a King who would rule on earth and overcome all the enemies of the Jews. This mom expected that one day Jesus would rightfully claim his kingdom, and she wanted her sons on either side of the throne when he did.

"Are your sons able to take the suffering I'm about to take?" Jesus asks.

James and John are nearby. They answer in unison, "Yes."

Jesus pulls James and John close for a teaching moment. Their answer indicates they have no idea what it means to carry your cross, and they have no idea what they are asking of Jesus.

> Jesus called them together and said, "You know that the rulers of the Gentiles lord it over them, and their high officials exercise authority over them. Not so with you. Instead, whoever wants to become great among you must be your servant, and whoever wants to be first must be your slave—just as the Son of Man did not come to be served, but to serve, and to give his life as a ransom for many."
>
> Matthew 20:25–28

Jesus came to care for others.

James the Elder doesn't know it yet, but his new faith was not designed to elevate him to a position of favor. He's in training to be a servant. Over the next handful of years, James will watch Jesus show God's love through one-to-one, hands-on personal sacrifice as he opens blind eyes, heals the decaying skin of lepers, and protects a fallen woman from the raised hands of men holding large stones. Jesus will walk into a bed of nails and wood to suffer and die so that James—and every generation thereafter—will know the love of the Father.

Faith isn't a position of favor. It's a posture of servanthood.

What is the heart of God? The Bible speaks more than seventy times about taking care of the widow. In nearly fifty additional passages, orphans are mentioned, with a call to not let them fall through the cracks of society. Then there are the Scriptures that remind us to protect the fatherless. When we glimpse the Father's heart, we can't help but find widows, orphans, and the fatherless.

God *loves* them.

He *defends* them.

He *commands* us to care for them.

He *opposes* the harm of them.

If James and John's faith is only to seek favor, they miss the heart of God. In fact, they miss the point completely. James will gain a special place beside Jesus on earth. That position won't lead to riches. He'll live in common with others and his basic needs will be met, but not much else. He'll quickly find that following Christ isn't about living a safe and comfortable life void of sacrifice.

Yet he is blessed beyond belief.

Perhaps these words contradict what you've been taught about faith. After all, if we ask for it, we receive it, right? Those Scriptures (we'll talk about them later) have nothing to do with our comfort; they are about receiving knowledge, wisdom, assurance, peace, and other gifts that carry no monetary measure. God does promise to meet our needs, but he clearly defines those differently than we might.

Perhaps reading this chapter makes you a little nervous. When I began to fully explore the heart of God, it caused me to pause. *That's not me, right? I'm not James, pushing for favor.*

I don't demand a comfortable life . . . or do I?

I don't expect favor . . . except for the times I really, really want it.

Come to Me

Surrendering Favor-Based Theology

When I consider Ashley and Andrew's question, I wonder if I'm brave enough to ask it: God, *is there something you're asking me to do?*

> Lord, sometimes when I see a need, I'm not sure what
> to do about it. I want to be wise, but also sensitive to
> your leading. Show me your heart and my part to play.
> —Suzie

What if I ask that question and it requires big sacrifice?

What if it leads me far from my comfortable plans?

What if loving others is a challenge?

When Jesus hung on the cross, I wonder if James held his head in shame over such a self-serving promotion by his mom years earlier. It's human nature to want favor.

God gave me favor.

Have you heard those words spoken? Have you said them yourself? I think we all have. Maybe you sensed God's favor when a prayer was answered, or when everything seemed to be going wrong but then started looking up.

Favor is scriptural. Joseph found favor in the dark recesses of a prison after being unfairly accused (Genesis 39:4). No matter how bad things became for him, he wasn't completely forgotten. He endured. Later, because it appeared that God was with him in the hardest places of his life, he was elevated to second in command under Pharaoh.

We can't equate that type of favor with finding the best parking spot when we have two good legs to carry us the distance. Sure, God cares about the smallest details in our lives—and there's nothing wrong with asking God to help us find our keys and giving thanks in the small things. The danger comes when our entire faith ideology is founded exclusively on what he offers us.

Listen to these words of A.W. Tozer:

In making Himself known to us He stays by the familiar pattern of personality. He communicates with us through the avenues of our minds, our wills and our emotions. The continuous and unembarrassed interchange of love and thought between God and the soul of the redeemed man is the throbbing heart of New Testament religion.[1]

Favor-based theology is me-centered theology. *What will you do for me? What is in it for me? If I do this, what will I receive in return?* When we shift away from that, our faith becomes less about us and more about knowing and responding to the heart of God.

Sometimes it's transforming to simply pause and ask these questions:

- Do I reflect on what might bring God joy?
- Do I seek to understand the deep longings of my heavenly Father?
- Do I ask him how I can connect with those longings?

For many of us, just broaching this subject makes us wary. We never want to topple into legalism or "I gotta do this to be a Christian." I promise you that's not where Jesus led the disciples. It's not a place I desire to linger.

God invites us to make a difference in an unjust world where children go hungry, where moms are addicts rather than nurturers, where teenagers are sold into sexual slavery, where children have no place to call home. It's an invitation to love in his name.

A dispute also arose among them as to which of them was considered to be greatest. Jesus said to them, "The kings of the Gentiles lord it over them; and those who exercise authority over them call themselves Benefactors. But you are not to be like that.

Instead, the greatest among you should be like the youngest, and the one who rules like the one who serves. For who is greater, the one who is at the table or the one who serves? Is it not the one who is at the table? But I am among you as one who serves.

Luke 22:24–27

As James followed Jesus, he observed him tipping the long-standing order of things on its head. In that culture, the older brother was always the boss. The servant was always the least. Children should always be kept quiet. Women were always lesser than men.

Not with Jesus.

Never with Jesus.

When you and I seek the heart of God over favor-wrapped theology, we become rabble-rousers too. We look beyond "what's in this for me" to join in Jesus' mission statement found in Luke 4:18–19. Andy Stanley, in *How to Be Rich*, says:

> I want you to help me reanchor the church to undeniable, mind-boggling, culture-shifting demonstrations of compassion and generosity. Generosity was the hallmark of the early church. They did for those who could not do or would not do anything in return. That was new. That got people's attention.[2]

Does generosity mark today's church? It certainly does, and it absolutely doesn't. We're the church, so it's easy to find those whose faith blesses them but doesn't reach much further. We also meet scores of believers whose faith is watching the broken mend or celebrating as the fatherless find an Abba Father. There are many wrapping their arms around the grieving widow so that she might experience the power of touch one more time. And then there are those like Ashley and Andrew, who delight the heart of the Father as they help the orphan discover what home feels like.

There Are a Thousand Different Ways to Love

Not everyone is called to adopt a severely special-needs child. Ashley says:

> I've also been told, "I could never do what you do." I actually like it when people say this because it gives me the chance to speak truth. And this is it: You are right. You can't do what God has asked me to do. And you shouldn't seek that or compare. This only sucks us dry and drives us away from the good things God has for your walk with Him. What I hope our life and obedience would lead others to is a longing to hold their lives, possessions, time, and futures with a very open hand before the Lord and to constantly be offering your all to Him.

Just last week I sat around the kitchen table eating tacos with a group of friends. I introduced Lovelle, a twentysomething who dropped by just to say hello. Lovelle was four when she went into the California foster care system. She lived in several different homes. When she was around eight years old, her grandparents brought her to live with them. It was the safest period of her young life. Then her grandfather was diagnosed with cancer, and her mother reclaimed her. Lovelle didn't remember much about her mom. All she knew was that when she was removed from the home at the age of four, little Lovelle was bruised.

Those bruises resumed. Lovelle was sexually abused by her mother's husband, and physically restrained and abused by both. When she was old enough, she left home, believing it was better to sleep on people's couches and to work as many jobs as necessary to support herself in order to be safe.

At the age of eighteen, she found a safe place in a ministry called Saving Grace. This residential home was started for girls who had aged out of the foster system or who had no safe place to call home. It was founded by Becky Shaffer, who had aged out of the system herself. Saving Grace offered structure and lots of love. While there, Lovelle met Holley, one of the mentors. When it was time for Lovelle to graduate from the sanctuary of Saving Grace, Holley approached her.

She asked if she and her husband could adopt Lovelle.

Lovelle was twenty-one years old.

The adoption process was simple and beautiful. Lovelle celebrated her first real Christmas. She had a place to go on Sundays for dinner. She married later that year, and her adopted dad walked her down the aisle. One day, when she has children, there will be a set of loving grandparents.[3]

As Lovelle shared her story, one of the women around the table said, "I want to be adopted."

She's fifty-two.

As an adoptive grandma, I understand the beauty. When I look at my grandbabies, all are instinctively loved because of who they are. Adoption is opening your heart to someone who doesn't have your DNA.

When my fifty-two-year-old friend said that she wanted to be adopted, another woman leaned over and said, "We're your family." She pointed to the women sitting around the table. "We are all your family."

There are a thousand different ways to be a family to the fatherless, the widow, and the orphan. There are the larger ministries like Saving Grace or 99 Balloons, and these were founded by women just like you and me with the hope of making a difference. Then there are those who integrate it in other ways into their daily lives.

One supports a single mom's ministry, showing up to rock babies while a group of single parents encourages one another.

Another family sacrificially gives each month to an organization that educates a child in poverty. One picks up women who have no cars and want to come to church. Another opens her home on Friday nights to teens whose home lives aren't ideal. Yet another sends handwritten cards to those who experience loss.

The temptation is to wait until the perfect moment or when our finances are in perfect order or when our home is perfectly clean. We're waiting for something BIG to come to us or to be in a right position to do something BIG ourselves. But all Jesus asks is that we care for a human being on his heart. In *How to Love Your Neighbor Without Being Weird*, Amy Lively says:

> [Loving your neighbor is] His second most important priority and His plan to reach the world with the Gospel, one neighbor at a time. Just ask Him *how*.[4]

A young mom in my church has young children, and when she was asked to mentor a college-aged girl, she struggled to say yes. Most days she's in her yoga pants, with no makeup and her hair in a ponytail, doing laundry and feeding young children. What good could she do in the confines of her toy-strewn life?

It was exactly those ordinary details that felt like mercy to the college student. Together they folded laundry, laughed, and sat around the table and talked at dinner. They took the kids to the park and played. She felt part of a family. Later this woman expressed how grateful she was that she didn't allow an overflowing laundry basket to knock her out of partnering with God.

The heart of Christianity is about collecting— not things, but people.

It's less about the task and more about the question "God, is there something you want me to do?"

The Reality of Partnering With God

Ashley and Andrew filled out endless paperwork. There was no definitive timeline, or an indication that it would all work. There were moments they felt helpless at the red tape. Almost exactly a year passed between the beginning of the process and traveling to Ukraine to meet their daughter in April 2013. They brought their oldest daughter, Madeline, with them and left the two younger in care of loving friends and relatives. Upon arrival, they planned to officially receive their referral and then live for six weeks in Ukraine before Paulina was released to them. Jet-lagged and excited, the couple sat and listened to what felt like an endlessly long conversation in Russian at their first meeting. It was clear that something was not right. The facilitator leaned forward. "I'm sorry. There's a mistake in paperwork. Paulina isn't eligible for adoption."

They were told to choose a different child or go home.

Ashley couldn't speak or think. She was devastated. She and Andrew chose to see Paulina regardless. They traveled for ten hours in a van while Madeline slept on Ashley's lap. Pursuing the heart of God was turning out to be harder than they thought it would be.

When they arrived, the staff at the orphanage emphasized that they wouldn't be taking Paulina home. It's what she expected, but that's when Ashley crashed. She was fatigued. She missed her little ones back home. She was in a strange place and nothing was in her control. She was in love with a little girl who wasn't going to be hers.

"I had worked it all out with God, you see. We had made plans. I felt deflated and devastated and unsure of what to pray," Ashley says.

From the beginning Ashley and Andrew had asked, "Is there something you want me to do?" That question had led to this orphanage—that she was certain of. Nothing was happening the way she thought it would. Ashley had two choices: to be angry and walk in fear, or to talk to him, turn to him, and trust.

She sat in the van and expressed every last bit of her fears, anxieties, and disappointment. And she cried. The van was a safe place to cry and cry. Whether it was with her and Andrew or with someone else, she longed for this little girl to find a home. She prayed the verse that she and Andrew had prayed over Paulina for months (see Psalm 12:5): "'Because the poor are plundered and the needy groan, I will now arise,' says the Lord. 'I will place her in the safety for which she longs.' Arise, Lord!"

Ashley says, "The circumstances as they were, or the bettering of the circumstances, were not the end nor proof of God's power and ability for us. My dependence on him and transforming more to his likeness, those were the reasons we took the road to Paulina."

The next day they finally met her. When they walked up the stairs of the orphanage, there she was. Just a foot away. Andrew, Ashley, and Madeline walked to the crib, and Ashley placed her hands on the sweet little body and said hello for the first time. She lifted her in her arms, held her close, and whispered, "I'm your mama, and I love you."

She knew that Paulina could not understand the words, but it was what she felt in her heart. For the next thirty minutes they were able to hold her, talk with her, and laugh.

When they returned to the van, they received a phone call.

The *nos* were miraculously turning into *yeses*. Things they were told would take months had taken hours. The people who initially told them to go home signed the paperwork and approved the adoption of Paulina.

I asked Ashley if I could share her story because I know her. Paulina has been with this family for two years now. The road to Paulina didn't end with bringing her home. It continues today.

Ashley says that parenting Paulina turned every single thing she thought she knew about parenting on its head. With three little ones, she was used to some semblance of control. *Do this; don't do that. Come here; go to bed.* When Ashley's babies cried, she generally knew why and could comfort and soothe that child. When they couldn't sleep, she rubbed their backs until they were calm. Now all that Ashley thought she knew and was good at had been traded in for a blank slate.

Paulina has medical issues that have landed her in the hospital multiple times. For the first eighteen months she was home, she woke up in the night screaming. Paulina couldn't communicate, and nothing Ashley tried seemed to help. It was heartbreaking and maddening. Paulina loved to put things in her mouth. In her previous world, Ashley could say no and her child would generally listen. With Paulina, she discovered she could say it a thousand times and it wouldn't register. Ashley learned that she couldn't control Paulina, which was humbling. She says, "It's taught me that I can do nothing for my children outside of Jesus. I need his strength daily to meet each of their needs, both tangibly and emotionally. And my dependence on him I pray will draw them to him as well."

There have also been miracles. Paulina's first word. The first time she ever sat in a chair. The first time she stood with the help of her daddy and a good set of braces. She has a smile and a giggle that are infectious. Her siblings love her a lot. Ashley calls her an outward picture of the gospel. Paulina carries her disabilities on the outside while others can hide theirs on the inside. Some people say that Ashley and Andrew are brave or good for bringing her into their family. Ashley says they are neither.

Being brave or good can only carry you so far. Life is too hard and too complex for trusting in that. What I would say is that we have an ache inside us to never be content outside the will of God being played out in our lives. It's an ache that leads me to throwing my hands up and shouting to God, whatever you want I am in. Hard for us has brought us our daughter, and she is an unbelievably good gift.

Don't Compare Your Road to [Fill-in-the-Blank] With the Roads of Others

Lysa TerKeurst created a foundation to build renewable energy sources for women in Africa and other third-world places. Ann Voskamp provides funds for food, shelter, and education for women rescued from ISIS. Christine Caine, through her A21 Campaign, frees women and children who have been sold into the sex-slave trade.

Perhaps you are like these women. Don't be afraid to dream big and unite your heart with God's!

Maybe, like me, you're not Lysa. You're not Ann. You're not Christine.

As I sought the heart of God, I wondered if I was doing enough. I told God that I'd go anywhere, that I'd do anything, and I felt a quick rebuke. There are those times that God chastens us in corrective love. This was one of those times. He reminded me that he had led me to Arkansas to love a handful of fierce, strong women battered by life.

It's not about the size of the serve. It's the willingness to do what he asks.

If I compare it with Ann's or Lysa's or Christine's ministries, it might seem like just a weekly Bible study with some snacks—except for the fact that each of these women matters to God, and this is exactly where I am supposed to be.

In God's economy, the thousands are just as important as the few.

The few are just as important as the one.

The one is why he came.

Because he *cares*.

TAKING IT DEEPER

1. Read Luke 10:29–37. What is one word to describe the neighbor in this story?

2. If there are a thousand ways to love others in his name, what is one that lights you up?

3. Why is it so easy to adopt a favor-based religion? Describe one way that it might show up in your own life.

4. We can't love every person. We can't meet every need. No one person is big enough, and it could lead to burnout. How do we find the heart of God in our own ministries, family, or life?

5. Put a face and a name to the words *fatherless, orphan,* and *widow*. What is one need, large or small, that this person might have?

6. Describe a time that someone loved you in his name.

7. What does James 1:27 teach us about faith?

8. "Is there something you want me to do?" Write these words down on a heart-shaped piece of paper. Place it where you can see it for the rest of the week. Don't try to make this happen, just let the question soak in.

SCRIPTURE

"When you give a banquet, invite the poor, the crippled, the lame, the blind."

Luke 14:13

PRAYER

Lord, show me the deep longings of your heart. If I have made my relationship with you one-sided, forgive me. Today I put my feet on a new path. I'm reaching for your hand. I want to live with a generous spirit in whatever way you lead.

LIVING AS A DISCIPLE

• Ask God to show you the longings of his heart.
• If a person comes to mind, show him or her God's love in one small way.
• Ask God to show you/your family your unique part in that mission.

4

Loving People You Don't Want to Love

The Bible tells us to love our neighbors, and also to love our enemies; probably because generally they are the same people.

G. K. Chesterton

My dad stands at five foot six and wears a size 6½ shoe, but when my siblings and I talk about him, you'd think he was Goliath. We have stories, like the time Dad was walking the dog in the neighborhood and the dog stopped to sniff the grass. A neighbor came barreling out of his home and said, "Hey, don't let that dog do his business on my lawn."

My dad's fists curled, ready to take on the taller man in a New York minute.

The man quickly went back into his house.

Then there was that time my sister's boyfriend got beat up. I was standing in the front yard when the light blue Volkswagen Bug roared down the street. The car jerked to a halt at the curb. My sister piled out of the passenger seat. Another car raced behind them. Two guys jumped out and started pummeling my sister's boyfriend through the car window. They dragged him out and jumped on him. Arms flailed. Feet kicked. I thought he was going to die. At all of thirteen years old, I didn't have a lot of skills, but I was fast. I ran into the house shouting for help. "Call the police!" I said. "He's dying. He's going to die!"

My dad calmly picked up a gun (he hunted and fished and collected old guns) and walked past me. Bam. Bam. Bam. Bam! Dad stood in the front yard of our modest suburban home, peeling off shots into the air until he had their attention. The attackers raced to their car. They were never seen again.

We learned early two lessons that dad was proud of teaching:

Never take crud from anyone.

Don't put up with nonsense.

I had to reword these two lessons because the originals weren't phrased quite so properly by my father.

I love this man fiercely. My dad married my mother when I was nine months old. He took on two little girls and loved us as his own. When he hugs me and says, "I love you, babes," I feel safe. He's a good man with a good heart, but from a young age he had to fend for himself. He survived by being tough.

Loving your family? Yes. But the thought of loving difficult people isn't on his radar.

Recently, I listened as these and other stories were shared at a family get-together. There were a lot of laughs as story after story topped one another. As I listened, I couldn't help but see the glimmering threads of those early lessons.

Live on the defensive.

Hand it to them before they get to you.

Strike one, you're out.

The person with the quickest fists wins.

When the Holy Spirit probes in my own heart, I have to admit that when I became a believer these were some of my greatest battlegrounds. I had to figure out what to do with these ingrained lessons, because they conflicted with Jesus' teachings such as "Love your enemy" and "When someone takes your cloak, give him your tunic too" (see Luke 6:27–29).

And when Jesus said, "If someone slaps you on one cheek, turn the other," whoa, I could hear my dad grunt at that. You don't ever let someone lay a hand on you. No way, no how!

Loving difficult people can be a struggle. As the saying goes, life is too short to spend time with people who are a pain. But what if the difficult person is your own child? What if it's your co-worker? A friend? Your spouse? A neighbor? What if God's calling you to ministry where difficult people will be in the mix?

And what if you're the difficult person? (Gasp!) We may not realize how our inability to love difficult people translates to the lack of grace we offer ourselves.

Let's take it deeper, because that's where Jesus leads the disciples. He asks the disciples to love difficult people—because difficult people matter to God.

How does that change us?

We can *choose* to live on the offensive and love them before they love us. We can give up the need to control that person or the situation. We can stop looking for flaws in others, because we realize how deeply flawed we all are. We can tear down walls a mile high and let people in with a measure of grace and lots of wisdom. Instead of responding to difficult people with a verbal karate chop, we can love them extravagantly. We can choose to no longer believe that "getting them before they get you" somehow makes us stronger.

None of this is easy, because these are the harder paths of faith. Loving difficult people is ripe with potential to show others God's love, but it's also where his greatest work begins in our own hearts.

Let's Sit With Simon the Zealot

Simon, also called the Zealot, stands in the crowd when Jesus calls out Matthew's name as an apostle. It's not hard to imagine what Simon is thinking, because choosing Matthew is a sacrilege. Seconds later Jesus calls out Simon the Zealot's name, which presents a challenge.

Follow Jesus. *Yay!* Serve side by side with Matthew? *Um, no.*

Scholars debate why Simon is called the Zealot. The religious sect known as the Zealots weren't fully organized until four decades after the gospels were written. Zealots were trained to believe that violence and overcoming the enemy were the only way to respond to unfairness. They were deeply religious men devoted to justice, but also rash in their hatred for Romans or anyone who dared to consort with Rome. Zealots wanted nothing more than to live in a free country uncontrolled by outside influence. Considered generous in good works, they were also known to liberally dispense violence (even murder) if it got the job done.

Was Simon an early convert to this belief system? Many religious and political movements stir underground for years before emerging publicly. Some Scriptures refer to Simon as Simon the Canaanite. This doesn't mean that he was from Cana. Rather, it's another word that translates to "zealot." Other scholars say that Simon was called the Zealot because he was zealous about his faith. In this time period, such fervor would resemble that of Saul, who persecuted Jesus' followers in a desire to maintain the purity of the faith.

Let's go back to that moment when Simon hears his name called.

He accepts and begins to serve side by side with a man who is an enemy of everything he holds dear. But it gets worse. The next morning Jesus gathers the newly appointed disciples around him.

> "Blessed are you when people hate you, when they exclude you and insult you and reject your name as evil, because of the Son of Man. Rejoice in that day and leap for joy, because great is your reward in heaven. For that is how their ancestors treated the prophets."
>
> Luke 6:22–23

As I listen to these words along with Simon the Zealot, I can almost imagine my dad. As Jesus says "Blessed are you when people insult you," I hear my dad saying "Baaaah!" It's a cross between a growl and a grumble, and it's what he says when he disagrees and wants you to know how foolish he thinks it all is.

For Simon the Zealot, this is a hard place. Jesus has already let a scoundrel into the Twelve. Now he's saying that to be insulted and rejected is an honor. All of this goes against the ingrained teaching of any good Zealot.

Over the next three years Simon watches as Pharisees taunt and try to trick Jesus with their questions. He is there when Jesus takes a beating that he doesn't deserve. He watches Jesus die on a cross.

How many times did Simon the Zealot curl his fists in anger? How many times did he follow Jesus instead of fighting back?

Jesus changed the name of a few of the disciples to reflect their true character, but he never changed Simon the Zealot's name.

I love that. To be a man of zeal is to be passionate. Simon was passionate to the very end. He lived longer than any of the other disciples. He traveled long past his senior years to share the news that Jesus is the Messiah. His passion remained kindled.

There are conflicting reports about his final days. Most historical accounts say that Simon the Zealot was sawn in two, giving his life for his faith.

Zeal (or passion), when laced with faith, doesn't need brute strength to deal with difficult people, for loving God and loving others is the substance of faith.

Come With Me

Loving Others Who Disagree With Us

What if we made it to the end of our life having loved only those who loved us back? My pastor asked that question one Sunday morning. Don't you hate it when the sermon feels like it was written just for you?

I don't want to live a safe life, where I surround myself with people who only believe like me, who look and sound like me, who agree with everything I say. But difficult people? I don't want to go out of my way to hang out with them on a regular basis, either. The occasional encounter is okay. I can do that. I learned a long time ago that with a smile and a gentle word (Proverbs 15:1), I can smooth over almost any uncomfortable situation. In most cases, the other person's crankiness has little to do with me and more to do with the burden they are carrying.

But that person who gets under my skin, who makes me want to leave a room, who questions or pokes at me, or who strongly disagrees with me and pummels me with words to make me think the way he does? That person I come in close contact with because she's a co-worker or neighbor—or a loved one?

That's a lot harder.

Blessed are you when people hate you, when they exclude you and insult you and reject your name as evil because of the Son of Man.

How do these words impact us in a real world? These are the questions I asked as I walked with the Twelve. They consistently encountered people who rubbed them the wrong way. Some were the Pharisees, but some were family.

> After this, Jesus went around in Galilee. He did not want to go about in Judea because the Jewish leaders there were looking for a way to kill him. But when the Jewish Festival of Tabernacles was near, Jesus' brothers said to him, "Leave Galilee and go to Judea, so that your disciples there may see the works you do. No one who wants to become a public figure acts in secret. Since you are doing these things, show yourself to the world." For even his own brothers did not believe in him.
>
> John 7:1–5

Danger lurks in the shadows of Judea, and Jesus' brothers are mocking him. Pushing all the wrong buttons because he's the guy who played big brother their whole life, and now he's saying he's the Messiah.

Jesus' response wasn't sugar sweet or fake. He didn't allow their difficult behavior to sidetrack him from the business of the Father.

It's not time yet, guys.

Then he went on with the business of his heavenly Father.

How do we do the same? The emotional instinct is to fight back or to make the other person see it the way we do. Perhaps

Father, this is my issue. I want to debate with those who are debating. My fingers itch with the desire to set them straight. I'm no different. Lord, help me to be discerning. To speak truth when it might be heard. To hold back words that only inflame or make me feel better. Help me to hold a conversation over finger-pointing. Let me show love rather than just talk about it.

—Suzie

we fight back on Facebook, or we try to get other people on our side.

Yesterday I unfollowed ten people on Facebook. I hope I'm not the only one who does this. Our nation is facing several pressing decisions in politics and other areas, and many have been responding with harsh words or generalizations. My newsfeed was filling up with trolling and debate. Hundreds and thousands of people who have no idea what Christianity is about watch these interactions as they spread like wildfire through cyberspace.

We are not without a voice—thank goodness for that. But let's picture how this social media drama might look in real life. Would we stand face-to-face in the grocery store or at the dinner table of a neighbor yelling our opinions, or would we hold a conversation? A colossal shouting match rarely changes anyone's mind. Generalizations that fail to address the person standing in front of you are damaging. Harsh words "in the name of Jesus" are impossible to take back.

So what *do* we do?

Our first step is to become acutely aware that Jesus loves us right where we are. He loves us when we are prickly. He loves us when we fail to think before we speak. He loves us on the day we yell at our kids and hang our head in shame. He loves us when we lose our cool in the car and show the car behind us who is boss. As hard as it is to understand, he loves us even when our behavior reflects poorly on his name. In that love, he speaks truth and leads us to a place of conviction and transformation, wrapped in mercy. It's a secure place that acknowledges that we are sometimes the difficult ones, yet we are safe with him.

Being loved by Jesus allows us to love others.

A response that grows out of being loved by Jesus is washed in mercy and truth rather than passive-aggressiveness (or just plain ol' aggressiveness).

There were numerous times that Jesus preached with few or no words. In Luke 6:6–11, a man walks into the temple. His right hand is withered. Jesus is teaching and Pharisees are watching. They know that Jesus is a do-gooder.

> Then said Jesus to them, "I will ask you one thing: Is it lawful on the Sabbath to do good or to do evil, to save life or to destroy?
>
> Luke 6:9 NKJV

After this handful of words, he asks the man to stand and come forward. Jesus restores his hand as whole as the other. His response was truth-based: *I don't agree with you, but let me show you what I mean.*

It didn't change their minds, but it spoke volumes to the man who couldn't work because his hand was dried up and useless. It impacted the family of that man. It convinced many in the crowd that Jesus was the Messiah. Jesus didn't try to change the minds of those who firmly believed they were right.

His entire focus was to go about the Father's business.

Are we prepared to do the same, whether that is on Facebook, with our neighbor, or with that teenager in our home who disagrees with every word that comes out of our mouths?

Loving People Who Really Are Difficult

Jesus was a yes-man, but not in the way we usually use that word. His yeses were to His heavenly Father, especially where it concerned people. Remember how he forgave Peter after he rejected Jesus three times in Jesus' hour of greatest need?

Even knowing this, there are still times that I want to completely walk away when someone hurts my feelings. I want to take a stand. I want them to say they are sorry—and mean it.

> Always be prepared to give an answer to everyone who asks you to give the reason for the hope that you have. But do this with gentleness and respect, keeping a clear conscience, so that those who speak maliciously against your good behavior in Christ may be ashamed of their slander. For it is better, if it is God's will, to suffer for doing good than for doing evil.
>
> 1 Peter 3:15–17

- Do I factor mercy into my response to those who hurt my feelings?
- Are my words laced with gentleness and respect?
- Do I take their harsh words and nurture them until bitterness takes root?

For most of us these are difficult questions because they are about ourselves, not the person who was unfair or unkind. Not too long ago, I had a difficult conversation. She had texted earlier in the day informing me that she wanted to speak with me.

The day before, she had asked me to help her with something, and I genuinely could not.

When we spoke, her words didn't accurately depict me or the situation. She told me that I helped others, but I wasn't there for her. She said that I wasn't a good friend. Her words weren't accurate, and it made me think of all the times I had been there for her. It hit a tender spot. You know, that one that says, "This is unfair." While I believed that I hadn't done anything wrong, I had ample opportunity to do wrong in my response.

Standing strong doesn't mean you step on others.

I could take a stand, or I could step into mercy.

I once took a marriage and family class, and the instructor, a licensed professional counselor, described a scene: A child stands in the freezing cold. She has no mittens and no hat, and her shoes are worn. She rings the doorbell and you answer.

"What is your reaction to this child?" he asked us.

Every last person in that class reacted in mercy. We brought her in out of the cold. We warmed her hands by the fire. We gave her steaming hot chocolate.

"Let's look at what you didn't do," he said. "You didn't stand at the door and scold her for being cold. You didn't yell at her for not having mittens. You didn't berate her for not wearing a hat. You didn't demand that she tell you where her parents were or why she wasn't at home where she belonged. Your first instinct was to bring her in from the cold. Then later you'd work through the details."

He likened this example to relationships in a difficult stage. He said that many of us leave each other out in the cold, hurting and in need, while we argue about how they got there. What a powerful lesson, one I've never forgotten.

I've imagined that child standing in the cold when I've had a difficult conversation with my husband, one of my grown children, or a friend.

It served me well that day on the phone. She genuinely felt hurt, and I was somehow linked to that hurt. She stood on the threshold in the frigid air of pain and anger. Listening allowed me to hear that hurt. It opened the door to talk through the details with honesty.

It wasn't an easy conversation, and everything didn't magically become perfect, but it did allow us to talk. It led me to respond (rather than react). It gave us an opportunity to share our individual points of view and work toward resolution. It helped me to understand where her hurt was coming from and why she felt the way she did. Others had let her down many times, and she thought I was becoming one of those people. It wasn't true, but that doesn't mean that it didn't feel true to her.

I hate conflict. Do you? Yet it will take place.

Bring them in from the cold.

That slight shift in perspective might even allow us to discover why that person is standing in the cold, why they are ill-prepared, or how they came to be at the door in the first place. If it doesn't, and it might not, then it changes us. We become vulnerably strong.

What Is Vulnerable Strength?

Vulnerable strength is flexible strength. It means not always having to be right. It means assuming that the other person might see it a different way. Even when you disagree, you don't throw verbal rocks. If someone did wrong, that doesn't make *you* weak. It's not a reflection of your inner character.

Vulnerable strength means that if the neighbor asks me not to let the dog do its business on his lawn, I am generous in my response. It's not the battle I choose to fight that day, because there are plenty of battles that are far more important.

If the enemy can rob me with such an inconsequential moment, then I'm going to be helpless in the bigger stuff. Vulnerable strength believes that God will give you wisdom to sort through where you should fight for justice or fairness. There will be times when evil needs to be confronted or wrongdoing addressed, but you don't have to fight every battle. In her memoir, *Undone*, Michele Cushatt says:

> We spend years restoring worn antiques, hundreds of dollars repairing wrecked and dented cars. But if a relationship sustains damage, we're more likely to relegate it to the scrap heap than try to restore its shine. We're far more enduring with our valuables than the people we claim to value. As a result, we accumulate junkyards filled with harsh words, hurt feelings, and damaged relationships. We toss people to the side, punish them for their fallibility. But eventually the wreckage grows beyond our ability to disguise.[1]

Vulnerable strength means that we stop living with our fists curled, and instead seek the heart of Jesus where people are concerned.

Loving People Who Are Different From You

Jesus threw cultural taboos to the wind as he dined with sinners and talked with sinful women in the public square. He loved them even as he pointed out their need for change.

I struggled with whether to include the story I am about to share with you. I took it out. I put it back in. I took it out. I put it back in.

I struggled for two reasons. One, it's a deeply private story, and sharing it with you means that it's open for debate. Second, I struggled because the person I am referring to in this story is gay. For many in the Christian community, this is a dividing topic.

If you wonder if I know what the Bible says about homosexuality, I do. It says the same thing about this as it does other sins. *Don't do it.*

I also know what the Bible says to all of us who have sinned. *Come to me. Let me change your life.*

I hope you'll listen to this story as if you were that thirteenth disciple, watching Jesus love people that infuriated the religious.

A friend agreed to go to a church service, and I was excited. He was moving toward Christ with a hunger so deep it was evident. We met on a Sunday morning and went in to the service. I prayed that the words spoken that day would resonate. After a powerful time of worship, the speaker stood to share his sermon. This was someone I really respected. I had seen him weep with addicts and pray for men and women who had abandoned their families, their identities, or their purpose to embrace sin. He was honest about the devastation that sin holds, but he always led them back to Jesus with compassion.

So when the speaker shared that he had some words to say about a recent political decision made in our state, I held my breath. Over the next several minutes, people in the congregation around me stood to their feet and clapped, shouting

Lord, it's far easier for me to talk about loving unlovable people than to acknowledge that there are times I'm unlovable or difficult.

—Suzie

amen. The words "Adam and Eve, not Adam and Steve" rang out from the pulpit.

No. Not today. Not on this day.

I was sitting next to someone who longed to know Jesus.

Moments earlier I had sensed my friend opening up to the presence of God in that building. People greeted him warmly. He was responsive to the worship. Now I tangibly felt the sadness as he closed up.

It's not that we shouldn't talk about sin. We need to. It's not that the church isn't a place where sin is brought to an altar so that Jesus can make us whole. It is. It was that suddenly the sin of the person sitting beside me was bigger than those of us sitting in that crowd.

Tears streamed down my face.

To my right I saw a friend who was divorced and happily remarried. The Bible tells us that divorce is wrong. He had found forgiveness and restitution in his relationship with his children.

I saw another who was once an alcoholic, and now her life was on track. Our heavenly Father scooped her from a broken place and healed her heart.

I saw myself—a mom and wife and woman who is sometimes impatient. Who has lost her temper and wished that she could take back the angry words. A woman who has said or done things she regretted only to find hope and transformation in a God who never gave up on me. I was changed by that love.

Every last person in that room had been forgiven and changed by Jesus. I felt a barrier erected that said, "Change first; then you can be one of us." That wasn't the sign held in front of any of the rest of us when we walked through the doors of the church, hungry, seeking something more. The sign had read "Come in. Let me introduce you to Jesus. We love you. Jesus died so that you can become whole, no matter your sin. He'll change your heart if you open it to him."

I leaned over to my friend. "I'm sorry," I whispered.

"It's what happens, Suzie," he said. He reached for my hand. "It's okay."

Unbelievable. He was comforting me.

We parted ways after the church service, and I wept all the way home. My friend was seeking Jesus, and he found the opposite. Over the past few years, we have shared several honest discussions about the Bible. We've prayed together. He has asked hard questions, and I have been gently straightforward about what Scripture says, while holding out the truth that we all fall short (Romans 3:23).

Every one of us.

I shared this story because it happened and it broke my heart. To be vulnerable with you, I didn't know what to do about it.

Loving others who are different isn't limited to any one person or difference. We simply need to see people as Jesus did.

People are watching our lives and asking if Jesus is worth following.

Simon the Zealot wanted things to be different in his world too. Jesus showed him that true change comes when we cross the street rather than explain how much better our way is than theirs. Jesus showed him that when he chose Matthew. He demonstrated it the day he called one very sinful man down from a tree (Luke 19:1–10). He shared a powerful sermon the day he healed a woman tormented by seven demons (Luke 8:2) and when he touched the unclean leper (Luke 5:12). Jesus met each of them in the *midst* of their sin or differences. There were no instructions on cleaning up first. Instead, "Come with me" was just as powerful an invitation as it was for those who were all cleaned up on the outside.

Come with me, and you'll find what you're seeking. I'll do what you cannot do on your own.

Perhaps you loved this book until right now. Maybe you're saying, "Suzie, we aren't to compromise on Scripture," and you are correct. We are to examine all Scripture and explore how to live it in our everyday life.

"Love me with all your heart, your soul, your mind. Love one another as I have loved you" (see Luke 10:27).

Jesus was far harder on the religious than he was on the seeking or the lost. They had a great treasure, and his rebuke was for those who used that gift to hold themselves in higher esteem than those who didn't have it.

> Jesus answered them, "It is not the healthy who need a doctor, but the sick. I have not come to call the righteous, but sinners to repentance."
>
> Luke 5:31–32

Sin is sin, is sin, *is* sin. There is no higher or lower level in Scripture.

Our God is the answer for sin, and he knew that, which is why he came for us.

A few weeks later my friend called me. He had visited a different church. That morning's sermon was about the prodigal son. He had never heard such a beautiful story and was embarrassed by his reaction; he sat in the pew and sobbed. He tried to slip away quietly after the service ended, but the pastor caught up and put an arm around him.

"Are you the prodigal son?" the pastor asked.

My friend's response was, "I think I might be."

"Why was I crying?" my friend asked as we talked on the phone. "Was that Jesus?"

Yes, yes it was.

I'm watching from a distance as my friend explores his new faith. He shares Scripture on Facebook. He's reading the Bible for the first time with the hope that it might be for him. He's a work in progress, just like I was when I first became a believer.

Just as I would with any other friend, I'm not holding up a list of things *I* think he should do. Instead, I'm watching in awe as Jesus takes a roughhewn new believer and gently begins to peel away the layers to reveal the new underneath. He's got a lot to figure out and work through. I've asked him to shut out my voice and the voices of others who are a little unsure of his decision, and to get alone with Jesus and the Bible.

I can't wait to see what takes place as he does just that. It's not going to look like my version of what-should-happen-when, but I know this: The Word powerfully changes us. The presence of God, combined with that Word, leads us out of our used-to-be lives to discover the new. Do we love people who are different from us?

What Jesus says about love forced me to ask hard questions. The answers weren't always what I hoped they'd be, but they opened the door to honest evaluation and tangible change.

- Do I only surround myself with people who think like me, act like me, or believe like me?
- Do I say I love people who are different from me, but never invite them around the kitchen table?
- Do I love first and judge second?

- Before pointing out another's sin, is it with the realization that I have sinned and been forgiven?
- Is there a person or group of people different from me (because of race, socioeconomics, ethnicity, culture, politics, or any other difference) that I know little about but still have strong opinions about?

Charles Lee says this:

Jesus did not place a standard on the kinds of people he would love and care for. In fact, if he did have bias, it was towards those who were ignored, discarded, or undervalued.[2]

Maybe you fear loving people who are different from you because it might mean that you agree with or condone their sin. It's the exact opposite. We believe in the power of God's love. That's what led Jesus to cross the street.

He was doing the business of the Father.

Walking with the disciples in this messy business called "love your enemies" helped me to answer the question I shared earlier, the one my pastor asked that haunted me for weeks: What if I made it to the end of my life having loved only those who loved me back?

Taking It Deeper

1. Read Psalm 139:23–24. What happens when we allow God to search those deep places in our hearts?

2. What is your knee-jerk response to a difficult person (your instant, emotional response)?

3. In what way do you sense God asking you to respond differently?

4. Are you ever the difficult person in a relationship? Be honest with yourself. Write down those areas where you invite God to help you grow.

5. Describe one way you can take a stand without stepping on others.

6. Name one person or people group that you've avoided, for whatever reason.

7. Put yourself in their shoes. What does your response toward them show them about Jesus? Ask God what he wants you to do differently.

8. Suzie said, "We are not without a voice." Name one way that you can make an impact on culture. Does this reflect how Jesus impacted culture or people who disagreed with him?

9. Almost all of the rebukes by Jesus were for the faithful. Was it out of love for those individuals? Explain your answer.

SCRIPTURE

Do to others whatever you would like them to do to you. This is the essence of all that is taught in the law and the prophets.

Matthew 7:12 NLT

PRAYER

Father, lead me to mercy. Show me how to love those different from me. Thank you for wisdom and direction when dealing with difficult people. When I am that difficult person, thank you for loving me.

LIVING AS A DISCIPLE

- Bring that person in from the cold.
- Combine convictions with compassion.
- Get to know someone outside your inner circle.
- Invite someone to sit around your table for a meal and community.

5

Why Do You Believe?

The Bible encourages people to put their faith in God. Unfortunately, many people equate faith with a blind leap in the dark or wishful thinking. But the faith that the Bible requires is intelligent faith. It is neither blind nor irrational. Biblical faith is a committing trust with an object (God) who is worthy of our faith. No one is asked to sacrifice his intellect when he puts his faith in the God of the Bible.

Don Stewart, *The Ten Wonders of the Bible*

She poured out all her thoughts about Christianity, negative and positive, in an email that landed in my in-box.

Dear Suzie, do you not understand that a lot of people see your faith in such a negative light? Are you fundamental, moderate, or liberal? What do you think about Christians who use God's name to hurt people?

I felt the Holy Spirit tugging when I read her words. Her email was much longer, but it boiled down to the three questions above. For the next few weeks this stranger and I talked back and forth. I agreed with her that faith can seem complex when it is tangled in a to-do list or is misused, and that there is a human element to faith that can sometimes disappoint. But I also told her that I'd been privileged to witness how faith changes the world and the people in it.

If you see me on a Sunday morning, I'm watching people, like the young couple on the second row. He used to be an addict; she used to feel hopeless. Now they worship God freely, a child nestled between them. I notice the woman in the choir whose husband doesn't believe, but she loves him well. Her joy comes from family, but also through a deep connection with her heavenly Father. I see the extra-tall guy who's bald and wears a funky cap. He's so in love with Jesus that it's hard to deny. It spills out of him. It's God's work inside of them that describes why I love him so much. It's his work inside of me that does the same.

I didn't hear from her for a couple of weeks. As time passed, I believed that she'd moved on. Then another email came. "What do you mean when you say that God has worked inside of you?" she asked.

There have been times when I lifted my hands to worship in the bleakest parts of my life and true praise rang out—though there was nothing praiseworthy at the moment. That was because of my faith, not because I was strong. There have been moments when I felt his presence close and knew I was not alone. I know that God has transformed my life and continues to do so, even in the questioning parts.

More emails back and forth. They were sporadic. I was never quite sure if I answered her questions adequately, but she continued to ask them. In one of the final emails, she sent only one question: "Why do you follow Jesus?"

I cannot see my life without a relationship that changed me so completely.

That was my answer. I told her that I couldn't shake the truth that my life took a turn when I became a believer. That knowing him is a thread through every choice, every decision, every part of my existence, and I'm grateful for that. I told her that I'm far from perfect and I don't have all the answers, because the truth is that sometimes I fall way short. But knowing my Savior is what changed everything, and it continues to do so.

We parted ways shortly after that. I don't know the finality of what she did with our conversation, but I do know that we moved away from the hotbed questions in her first email to the personal joy of knowing Christ. In the beginning, she approached me because she didn't like aspects of the Christian faith as she understood them. As time went on, it was because she was genuinely seeking answers. In her last email she shared that she was praying. She had moved from asking me questions to asking God.

I can't help but find joy in that.

If this conversation had struck up twenty-five-plus years ago, I may have responded differently. I was not a new believer, but growing in my faith. I had been taught to tell others about Christ using tools like the Romans Road—a series of Scripture passages found in Romans, accompanied by questions a seeker might ask. I also had resources like tracts, small brochures that asked questions such as "Are you going to heaven?"

My email friend wasn't seeking the Romans Road and didn't want to read a tract. She didn't really want to know what to believe, but *why* a person would choose to believe.

Did you know that it's conceivable to be a believer and still struggle to answer that question? We may understand the concepts of our faith, or at least what we've been told. Perhaps we felt something at one time, or wanted to avoid something else, so the obvious choice was Christianity. Maybe going to church is something we've always done, or it makes us feel safe or has brought comfort in a hard time. Perhaps the thought of hell drove a few to their knees.

When someone asks us why we believe, it forces us to dig deep to answer that question. That's why the Romans Road or a tract or rehearsed questions might have been my response years ago. I'm not putting down those resources, because we do need to understand the powerful Scriptures behind God's beautiful gift. The problem is that most people aren't looking for a set of Scriptures that they might or might not grasp yet. The underlying question most are asking is, "Did those Scriptures do anything in you?"

It's an important question, and before we share the answer with anyone else, part of the adventure is to discover it for ourselves.

Spend the Day With John, the Beloved Disciple

John is the son of Zebedee and brother to James. He is the first chosen by Jesus as one of the Twelve. We rarely hear his name mentioned without Jesus being somewhere close by. We also get a glimpse of John's personality. Have you ever met someone who likes to remind you of how close they are to someone important? John reminds us four times in the gospel of John that he's the disciple that Jesus loves. It's a beautiful sentiment, but we never hear it from Jesus' lips.

Is this the "son of Thunder" (Mark 3:17) just showing off a bit, or is John the beloved disciple?

One day a quarrel starts among the disciples. They argue back and forth, trying to decide who is the greatest among them. Jesus overhears this argument and calls a little child to stand beside him. He wraps his arm around the child.

> "Whoever welcomes this little child in my name welcomes me;
> and whoever welcomes me welcomes the one who sent me. For
> it is the one who is least among you all who is the greatest."
>
> Luke 9:48

Later John sees a man driving out demons in Jesus' name, and it troubles him. He tries to stop him because he's afraid that this person is giving Jesus a bad name. He runs to Jesus and tells him what is happening.

> "Do not stop him," Jesus said, "for whoever is not against you
> is for you."
>
> Luke 9:50

In another instance, Jesus and the disciples set out for Jerusalem. When they arrive in a Samaritan village, the people don't welcome Jesus. That makes the disciples angry, especially James and John. The brothers ask Jesus if they can call fire down from heaven to destroy the unwelcoming bunch. Jesus rebukes them, and they go to the next village (Luke 9:55–56).

In each of these encounters, Jesus is showing John how to believe.

In the first two instances, Jesus is showing John that he isn't the star. He points to a child, one of those on the Father's heart. He reminds John that every member of the team counts, for when we work together, there's a greater chance that people are healed, that chains and bonds are broken in his name, and that the "least of these" are found.

And that last encounter where John wants to call down fire? Jesus isn't about to let John get caught up in emotion and start fires, leaving a burned-down mess that scorches rather than draws the villagers to truth.

We could spend days on these stories. They teach us how to practice our faith in real life. In every case, Jesus instructs John and then keeps going.

Come on, guys, we have things to do.

There's more to see. More miracles ahead. More growth to experience. More mountains to climb. The longer John walks with Jesus, the more he starts to understand why he believes.

Three years later, John is the only disciple who stands with Jesus as he is questioned, brutally flogged, and handed over to the crowd to decide his fate. John's family has ties to the high priest, Caiaphas, so he is able to be with Jesus. It was a dangerous decision to be there that day. When you stand in the shadow of an accused criminal as his support and friend, there's a good chance the spotlight will shift to you.

Hours later, as Jesus hangs on a rough, rugged cross, he asks John to take care of his mom.

This is where John's assertion that he's the beloved disciple starts to feel true. John risks his life to stand by Jesus. He is chosen by Jesus to watch over his mother. That's a job for someone you trust without reservation.

John lived many years after Jesus' death. He is the only disciple not martyred for his faith, but he did suffer for it. Most historical accounts report that John was boiled in oil, and at the end of his days he was sentenced to live in bleak isolation on the deserted island of Patmos.

> This is how we know what love is: Jesus Christ laid down his life for us.
>
> 1 John 3:16

John wrote these words as an old man, roughly eighty-five to ninety years after the death of Jesus. John was the second to last of the twelve original disciples to leave this earth (Simon the Zealot was the last). He knew why he was a believer. He loved Jesus to such a degree that he couldn't help but tell the world that he was the most beloved disciple of all. Here's where we gently land on a spiritual treasure.

When we finally come to know *why* we believe, we can't help but call ourselves his.

Come With Me

We Might Not Understand All of It at First

Sometimes the disciples seemed dense. We often hear Jesus saying things like this:

Pay attention.

Listen to my words.

Note this.

And when he really wanted to get their attention, *This is my commandment.*

He spoke in illustrations that might seem complex to us, but that made perfect sense in their culture and context. He punctuated lessons with stories. He gathered them around like a circle of preschoolers so he could see them eye to eye and pour into them. It wasn't condescending, but relational.

Three years into their relationship, however, the disciples still responded in this manner:

Lord, give me a sign.

Jesus, I think I know more than this guy.

I know you told me to do it this way, but I'm doing the opposite.

Savior, you asked me to stay aware, but I really want a nap.

> *Faith that is never questioned becomes a habit.*

They doubted. They questioned. They messed up. But they also believed . . . again and again until it became truth.

When we first step into our faith, it's uncharted territory. It's clear from Jesus' example with the disciples that he doesn't call us to follow only to leave us unaffected.

I loved the questions my email friend asked at the start of this chapter, because they made me fall in love with Jesus all over again. Everything I wrote her is true, and I don't want to take my faith for granted. As I reminded myself of why I believe so that I could share it with her, the wonder of my faith rose above the familiarity of it.

Whether you've been a Christian for fifty years or you picked up this book because you want to know *why* to believe, faith is like any beautiful relationship. It deepens over time.

The problem is that it can also fade. Faith that is never questioned becomes a habit. Faith that fails to go deeper has no roots when it's needed most (Matthew 13:1–9). Faith that tells everyone else what to do fulfills no one.

Chasing the "why" of our faith helps us to discover what Brennan Manning calls the furious longing of God:

> Because we approach the gospel with preconceived notions of what it should say rather than what it does say, the Word no longer falls like rain on the parched ground of our souls. It no longer sweeps like a wild storm into the corners of our comfortable piety. It no longer vibrates like sharp lightning in the dark recesses of our nonhistoric orthodoxy. The gospel becomes, in the words of Gertrude Stein, "a patter of pious platitudes spoken by a Jewish carpenter in the distant past."[1]

I don't know about you, but I have found myself standing vulnerable before him, my soul yearning for rain on the parched ground of my faith. I'm asking him to sweep into my comfortable faith like a wild storm. I'm kneeling before him, shamelessly asking that his Spirit vibrate in all the dormant and man-bent scars that dare to represent faith and fall short.

Whose faith is it anyway?

It's ours. It's personal. It's corporate, as well, as we worship with other believers. It's vast as we join with millions upon

I sometimes settle for far less in my faith than what is offered to me. Thank you that you teach us how to live our faith. Those practical parts that are real life. Thank you more for the personal and precious and powerful relationship we can have with you.

Light me up inside. Take my tired, burned-out religion and bring my relationship with God to life.

—Suzie

millions, from Jesus' day until now. But first, it's a one-to-one relationship with God.

We'll have lots of questions. The answers aren't going to be revealed all at once. In multiple instances the disciples didn't comprehend, but years later they were surprised as words or entire conversations came back to them. Their understanding came in layers. That makes perfect sense because that's how we learn about anything, but especially something as deep as our faith. The disciples would look around, amazed at what they had heard over and over again, only now to have clarity.

Then they remembered his words (Luke 24:8).

Only after Jesus was glorified did they realize that these things had been written about him and that these things had been done to him (John 12:16).

After he was raised from the dead, his disciples recalled what he had said. *Then* they believed the Scripture and the words that Jesus had spoken (John 2:22).

Martin Luther said, "The Bible is alive, it speaks to me; it has feet, it runs to me; it has hands, it lays hold of me."

That's how I see faith.

Then she believed that she was called.

After many years, she fully embraced his love.

Then she remembered his words.

Like John, *she realized* that she was utterly loved, which allowed her to love utterly.

It's Not Just About Skipping Out on Hell

Sitting in traffic, I was scanning through radio stations and landed on a Christian talk show. One of my favorite pastimes is listening to great preachers and teachers. I didn't have access to my downloaded podcasts, so I happily settled in to listen to the radio station until the host said these words:

"If there wasn't a heaven or hell, most people wouldn't follow Christ."

Josiah, my two-year-old grandson, mimics the expression I make when I'm shocked or surprised at something. It's one of my grown children's favorite amusements. "Hey, Josiah. Make your Gaga face." I'm certain that's the exact expression I made at the words I heard on the radio. I listened further because I wanted to understand where he was coming from. His point was that heaven is our reward and that our time on earth is fleeting. He said that we naturally desire sin, and the reward of heaven is the only thing that keeps us from giving in.

There were glimpses of truth, but it missed the greatest truth.

There's immense reward in serving Jesus right now, today, right where we are.

Calling yourself a Christian leads to death in many countries. We can't ignore the fact that believers are torn from their homes, forced to forsake Christianity, and killed or forced into slavery if they do not. The challenges that we face as believers in the United States pale in comparison.

That doesn't mean that faith is always easy. Scripture tells us to deny ourselves. We are instructed to love people we don't like. We are asked to forgive. We are told to store our treasures in heaven rather than accumulate it on earth.

We are asked to hold our tongues. To be honest. To submit—a word I didn't like for years until I understood the scriptural meaning (to yield to another). If we follow Jesus, that relationship will take us up harder paths while others around us seem quite happy to take the less bumpy road.

Certainly, faith isn't easy, but according to this radio preacher and perhaps in our own minds, staying on the straight and narrow is our task in life. Kind of like a chore. Or like clocking in every day and doing our deeds so that one day we can rake in our reward of retirement or a gold watch.

We miss a great deal if this is our belief system. There's the potential that our faith becomes drudgery. We put enough in so that we can get by, and after a time it feels so shallow that we're drowning in its emptiness.

I've felt this. It's what led me to walking with Jesus through the gospels. I've been a believer for four decades, and I love him with everything that is within me. But there are days I forget that the reason I call myself a believer is because I *believe* what is in the pages of the Bible—and more so, I believe that it's for me. If this is where you are as well, ask God to reignite your love for him.

> Until now you have not asked for anything in my name. Ask and you will receive, and your joy will be complete.
>
> John 16:24

Let's pause and pray this prayer together: *Father God, you tell us that you know what we need even when we don't have words to voice it. Surprise me with what you want to do inside of me. I want nothing less than all of you. I give you nothing less than all of me. In the beautiful name of Jesus, amen.*

Allow Jesus to Invade Your Personal Space

John lies next to Jesus around the table. In that day, they don't sit on chairs, but recline on the floor or mats or pillows with the food on low tables in the center. When I imagine doing the same with close friends, it makes me giggle. My friend Pam reaches over my shoulder for the fruit dip. Her husband, Jim, is head-to-head with Richard as they munch on turkey meatloaf and grilled zucchini skewers and talk about the Rangers game. It's a relaxed setting, but it's also close quarters.

Jim and Pam would be all up in my personal space. I would be in theirs.

Which is exactly what Jesus did with his disciples. This is what happens when we make our faith relational. We enter into his personal space and he occupies ours. We don't run the other way as the Holy Spirit digs far deeper than we are comfortable with. Instead, like taking an X ray of our inner self, we welcome him to reveal those areas that need his touch. We talk with him as we make decisions, long before we turn to anything or anyone else.

And when we want to call fire and lightning down on people who hurt our hearts or don't act like we think they should, well . . . instead of fighting against Jesus' rebuke, we learn from it and keep on going because we are a part of his plan to reach and love others.

There are mountains to climb. Miracles to experience. Things to explore and discover. For we are his beloved disciples.

TAKING IT DEEPER

1. Imagine a friend sitting across from you, a cup of coffee in front of each of you. Share with her a moment that Jesus became real for you.

2. What is the distinction between *what* and *why* you believe? Can you have one without the other?

3. John was the beloved disciple; are you? In one paragraph or less, describe why.

4. What does it mean to make your faith your own? How important is it, and why?

5. "There's immense reward in serving Jesus right now, where we are." What is your response to that statement? True or False?

6. Read John 12:37 and John 20:9. Contrast the difference between these two struggles with belief.

7. The disciples' faith matured in layers. How does this assure you in your own faith? How does it give you grace for others?

8. Regardless of why you first became a Christian, why are you a believer today?

SCRIPTURE

I will show what it's like when someone comes to me, listens to my teaching, and then follows it. It is like a person building a house who digs deep and lays the foundation on solid rock. When the floodwaters rise and break against that house, it stands firm because it is well built.

Luke 6:47–48 NLT

PRAYER

*Jesus, thank you that I am your beloved disciple. As
I sit at your feet, teach me. Let your words spring*

*to life inside of me and take root. May I live what
I believe in greater measure as I walk with you.*

LIVING AS A DISCIPLE

- Ask God to show you one person who is seeking him.
- Embrace the joy of walking with Jesus today.
- Invite God into your personal space. Step into his.

6

Believing Big When You Feel Small

Faith sees the invisible, believes the unbelievable, and receives the impossible.

Corrie ten Boom

A well checkup revealed something not quite right, and that led to tests and a biopsy. The doctor assured us that good news was more than likely, so we squeezed the doctor's appointment onto our calendar, which looked something like this:

Walk/jog.

Pray. Study.

Eat breakfast.

Go to doctor's appointment to hear good news.

Go back to work.

Unfortunately, good news didn't arrive. The biopsy revealed that Richard had cancer. We sat in the consult room stunned as the doctor tossed out words like *surgery* and *statistics* and *stage of illness*. I'll never forget the moment Richard asked a certain question. I could tell he was shaken, because it didn't totally make sense. The doctor laughed. Not the good kind, where you are laughing with someone. It was at him. My protective instincts went into full gear, and I wanted to push the doctor off his tiny roll-around chair. Richard leaned over and placed his hand over mine.

He knows me so well.

Misplaced anger wasn't welcome, and it wouldn't solve anything. There were more important battles ahead.

Again.

Twenty-four years ago, I found a lump when I was thirty-one. I convinced myself that it was harmless, so when I finally lay on the exam table months later, I discovered that I had waited too long. The lump was a tumor. The tumor was cancerous. The cancer had spread. For the next two years our lives were consumed with surgeries and chemotherapy and radiation and tests and more tests. I went through menopause before my mom did. The skinny girl who couldn't gain weight no matter what she ate put on nearly thirty pounds in the first month after surgery. There were times I didn't know who I was as I stared at my reflection. The woman standing there with newly added pounds, pale skin, and purple veins pulsing with toxins was a stranger. Those two years were frightening, but also a time of intense trust.

I thought about that as we stood in a parking lot, my arms around my guy.

My journey with the disciples was almost over. I had been traveling through Luke and the gospels for nearly a year. Jesus was as real as I had experienced him in a long time. So it was surprising that fear nearly toppled me. I closed my eyes, holding tight to the man who makes me laugh until I have to run to the bathroom. The man whose kindness and steady love are a gift to a girl once raised in brokenness.

The person I love second, after Jesus.

We hadn't budgeted time for much more than that embrace. Richard had clients waiting. Many of his therapy clients are children. It wasn't easy for their parents or guardians to get them there. It was important that he leave.

I had women arriving at my home in an hour for Bible study.

Richard and I promised to talk later that evening, then climbed into our respective cars and turned different directions on Interstate 49.

Crazy thoughts flitted in my brain while I drove. Silly things like the fact that I hadn't prepared snacks. Suddenly I realized that I couldn't see. I pulled off at the next exit and found a safe place to park. I rested my head on the steering wheel and wept like a baby.

Walking With Thomas

It's a shame that Thomas is permanently labeled as Doubting Thomas. That nickname sticks for years because of the famous incident on the day of Jesus' resurrection. Jesus appears in a room where the disciples are locked behind barred doors. They think he is a ghost, but he assures them that it's him, all right. It's Jesus, raised from the dead! Unfortunately, Thomas is the only disciple not in the room. He shows up a little while later, and the disciples excitedly tell him that Jesus appeared and talked with them. He replies like most of us would.

I can't believe it.

I need to see this for myself.

You see, the last time Thomas saw Jesus was when his broken body was lovingly placed in a barren tomb. He witnessed the brutal beating, the out-of-control crowd, the interrogation. He despaired as Jesus hung on a cross between two criminals. It seems impossible that Jesus could be alive.

Eight days later Jesus shows up again. He walks over to Thomas and holds out his hands. "Put your finger here; see my hands. Reach out your hand and put it into my side. Stop doubting and believe" (John 20:27).

We are invited to park our faith in the supernatural over the natural.

There's no harshness in these words. Jesus invites Thomas to replace natural doubt with evidence of the supernatural standing in front of him.

Jesus knows Thomas's character. Like the time that Lazarus is sick and Mary and Martha beg Jesus to make the trip to heal him. Many of the disciples try to persuade Jesus to stay away. The Jews have been plotting to stone Jesus. It is foolhardy to walk into danger. But Thomas says, "Let us also go, that we may die with him" (John 11:16).

Thomas isn't a doubter or weak in his faith. He's just a real person who is struggling to believe that a dead man has been raised from the tomb.

Jesus reaches out his hands, giving Thomas what is needed to believe "big."

I can look back and see times when I believed big—but many times when I wasn't sure how to believe at all. Not every prayer is answered in the way we want it to be. At other times we can almost mark the moment when the miraculous turned things around.

Should we believe in miracles today?

What does it mean to believe big, and what does faith in the supernatural look like in our generation, as opposed to three days after Jesus' death? I want to believe big, but the reality is that sometimes I feel really, really small.

Come With Me

The Miracle of His Presence

I made it home in time for Bible study. We gathered around the table and opened our Bibles, flipping to the Scriptures for the day's study.

I didn't tell them what had just taken place because I hadn't had time to process it myself. We hadn't told our children. I needed to talk with Richard more in depth. So I numbly read the passage in front of me. It was the story of the second miracle of fishes and loaves.

Jesus had multiplied a little boy's lunch into enough to feed thousands, with leftovers to take home for dinner that night. A few days later there is another opportunity. The crowd is just as big. Same problem as before. Too many people. Too little food. Not enough faith.

> About this time another large crowd had gathered, and the people ran out of food again. Jesus called his disciples and told them, "I feel sorry for these people. They have been here with me for three days, and they have nothing left to eat. If I send them home hungry, they will faint along the way. For some of them have come a long distance." His disciples replied, "How are we supposed to find enough food to feed them out here in the wilderness?"
>
> Mark 8:1–4 NLT

"What are we going to do?" the disciples ask.

Can you see it? Jesus shakes his head.

Seriously, guys? Really?

Or at least that's what I imagine.

I often write in the margins of my Bible. In bold letters I saw my own words staring up at me: *How did they forget the first miracle so soon?* The page blurred. I stood next to the disciples, except this time I was in a parking lot in Fayetteville, Arkansas, with my arms around my husband.

I had forgotten our first miracle.

Twenty-three years earlier, when I was sick with cancer, I felt his presence in the sterile, white room as I discovered that cancer was in my breast and lymph nodes. His presence cloaked us as we sat with our young children and tried our best to tell them that mama was sick. His presence was strong as I lay on a metal hospital gurney and was wheeled into surgery. It was there as I lifted my hands in worship when the doors shut behind me and Richard stood in the empty hallway, wishing he could be by my side.

We beat the odds, and that was a gift. For a long time I thought that was the big miracle, but later I realized the true miracles came as we dug deep into our faith and came up with enough to make it through the day—or the hour if that was what was required.

That was our loaves and fishes, multiplied beyond our meager supply.

My friends at Bible study didn't know what to think as I sat there, holding open my Bible, tears dropping onto the page.

I was Doubting Thomas standing in front of Jesus. He was holding out his hands. *Feel the wound in my side, Suzie. Touch the nail scars in my hands. I'm the same God who was with you then. I'm the same God now.*

When you and I are hard-pressed or shaken, or we have no idea what we're going to do because the problem is big and we're small, we're not alone. He's with us—stepping into the emotions that we experience to draw us closer to him. In *Women at the Cross*, author Linda Lesniewski explains it like this:

> Helplessness, guilt, anger, misplaced pity, and couldn't-there-be-some-other-way emotions can detour and distract our hearts. They can keep us from remembering that God will bring us through to a fresh, new, awe-inspiring understanding of his great love.[1]

It's easy to take his presence for granted, yet to be without it would be bleak. It's a supernatural miracle. He steps into our natural emotions, heartache, brokenness, doubt, and fear and makes himself known.

The Miracle of "Enough"

Jesus points to a group of men wearing long robes and carrying full bags of coins. Jesus and the disciples are in the Court of Women, not far from the beautiful gate. Thirteen horn-shaped vessels are placed around the open court in the temple. Offerings support the work of the temple. The men cast in their great sums. Jesus says,

> "Beware of the teachers of the law. They like to walk around in flowing robes and love to be greeted with respect in the marketplaces and have the most important seats in the synagogues and the places of honor at banquets. They devour widows' houses and for a show make lengthy prayers. These men will be punished most severely."

Luke 20:46–47

Some of the men who publicly give large amounts are the same men who pray long public prayers and wear their piety like peacock's colors. Some also privately take advantage of the most vulnerable.

Jesus directs his disciples' attention away from the men to a widow. She's a pauper, the poorest of the poor. A widow is at the mercy of others unless there is a man—a son, a father, a brother, a benefactor—to stand in support of her. The widow approaches the giving vessels and humbly puts in two farthings, a widow's mite, a grand total of one-hundredth of a day's wages. In contrast to almost anyone's offering, it's miniscule. When the money is counted later, this offering will account for little. Jesus saw it differently.

> "Truly I tell you," he said, "this poor widow has put in more than all the others. All these people gave their gifts out of their wealth; but she out of her poverty put in all she had to live on."
>
> Luke 21:3–4

Why is her offering greater? The wealthy have given out of their excess, while she has given out of her want.

This is our second miracle. Jesus meets us when we present him our *not enough*. The temptation is to shy away from God when our problem or the circumstance is big and we are small, because we feel we don't have enough to offer. We want bigger faith. A plan. Anything! We act as if it is our works or our efforts that please God. It's far easier to march in with our heavy purses filled with our overflowing faith or our overflowing confidence than it is to hold up our two farthings of doubt.

God doesn't want us to wait for our plans to fall into place before approaching him. He's not asking us to hold up our big moves and our big open doors, all tied up with our big confidence, and call it faith.

Faith is birthed in the trenches of our *not enough*. Jesus declared the widow's gift as greater because it was an act of trust. She surrendered *all* she had. She didn't compare her gift with the gifts of others. She didn't ask for an accounting of her offering. She just gave what she had and expected that it would be put to good use.

What Jesus sees as big is different from what we see as big.

There were times that the disciples begged Jesus to increase their faith (Luke 17:5–6). Have you ever done the same? Jesus assured them that if they had faith as small as a mustard seed, they could do great things—and that leads us to another spiritual swing in our thinking as disciples.

Surrendering all that we have from the very beginning is a big move of faith. It's running toward him with the anticipation that he already knows what's going on in our hearts and heads, and that he'll walk through it with us.

We give him our *not enough* faith.

We give him our *not enough* direction.

We give him our *not enough* talent.

We give him our *not enough* confidence.

We give him our *not enough* money.

We give him our *not enough* parenting skills.

We give him our *not enough* patience.

We give him our *not enough* [you fill in the blank].

This is where faith expands to include the supernatural. Over and over in Scripture, Jesus asks the disciples to give what they don't seem to have. It tests their faith, certainly. It shifts their focus from themselves—or their overflowing purses (or lack thereof) and their own natural giftings—to him.

I give you my <u>not enough</u> and trust that you can do immensely more with it than I can imagine. Today my <u>not enough</u> is all the very real details that come with cancer. Hospital bills. Tests. Uncertainty.

I'm afraid, God, 'cause this is my guy. I don't know why, but it was easier when it was me. I'm holding it all up to you.

—Suzie

When Richard was first diagnosed, I didn't have enough faith, and it's okay to acknowledge that. As long as I was willing to give him what I did have. Every hard place. Every strikingly beautiful moment. What does God want? All of it.

The widow's offering brought Jesus joy. Even if it seemed like not enough for the need at hand. When we give him our *not enough* it brings just as much delight.

The Miracle of Belief

Richard is healing. Just this morning he took his first run after eight weeks of recovery. In three more months we'll be back in the surgeon's office to determine how successful the surgery was for my guy. Through this process I carried my *not enough* to God on a regular basis. For whatever reason, the girl who was a rock during her own cancer wasn't nearly as strong when it struck the man she loved.

I wanted to be strong for Richard and my grown children and grandchildren, but it had to be more than an outward show. I found what I needed in the private moments, just God and me, where I held up my *not enough* and asked him for help.

The miracle of having belief is that we know where to go when we're in need. My most recent need was Richard's diagnosis. What is yours? Whatever big thing you are facing, God not only sees it, but is waiting for you. Step toward him with your hands raised high, no-holds-barred, bringing him every uncertainty, every hope, all your fears, all your strength, every aspect of your situation. The "big" is birthed inside of you as you believe that he can do something with the little that you do have. Whether it leads to a lame man leaping to his feet (healing), a few loaves multiplied by thousands (provision), hymns sung in the darkness of prison (hope), or standing near to Jesus while everything around you seems to fall apart (courage), your faith becomes an anchor as you find what you need *in* those hard places through him.

Our __not__ enough becomes more than enough when we give it to God.

Should We Believe in Miracles?

I experienced a miracle twenty-plus years ago, surviving an advanced cancer diagnosis. I've shared the story in another of my books, but the truth is that I struggle with sharing it. Others who prayed in faith went on to eternity. My faith wasn't any bigger than theirs. I wonder if, one day when I get to heaven and tell them about my extra time here on earth, they'll explain the glory of what they experienced by showing up a few years early.

Aside from my healing from cancer, I've experienced an even greater miracle—I was once a mess inside, and today I'm whole. So much so that I have forgotten what it feels like to be torn up from the inside out. That's a miracle that shows up not just in me, but in generations after me.

I have prayed prayers in faith and known without a doubt that God turned it around. I have also prayed prayers in faith and seen things turn out much differently than I hoped. We can hold tight to God in both situations.

I'm never going to stop believing in miracles, because if Jesus performed them, then they are possible today as well. Rex Rouis, who hosts HopeFaithPrayer.com, says, "Faith is hearing Jesus say, 'Come.' Believing is actually throwing your leg over the side of the boat."[2] I want to stand beside him when there are just five loaves and some fish and believe that they will feed a crowd. I desire to place my hands on people in faith and believe they'll feel Jesus' touch.

This is also my prayer: I don't want to fail to celebrate all the miracles I experience as his follower. Luke 1:45 says, "You are blessed because you believed that the Lord would do what he said" (NLT).

We are blessed as we soak in his presence when we cannot exist without it. We are blessed as we bring our *not enough* and it proves sufficient. We are blessed as we place a mustard seed of faith in his hands, and it grows—and we grow right along with it.

Taking It Deeper

1. Describe in a few words those circumstances or situations where you feel that what you have to offer is not enough.

2. What does it mean to believe big when you feel small?

3. Jesus invited Thomas to feel the nail prints and view the wound in his side. Why would he offer something so personal to the disciple?

4. The widow's mite was so little. How does our mustard seed of faith bring God joy?

5. Read Luke 21:4. Describe one way you might give out of your want rather than your excess?

6. In John 20:27, the word *faithless* or *doubt* means "don't be without trust." Is this a rebuke or an invitation? How do Jesus' words encourage you?

7. Share a story of a miracle (whether it is your story or someone else's).

8. Suzie described different types of miracles. Is any greater than the other?

SCRIPTURE

It is like a mustard seed, which is the smallest of all seeds on earth.

Mark 4:31

PRAYER

Jesus, I offer you my tiny seed of faith. Use this not enough *in great measure. Help me to believe big in you.*

LIVING AS A DISCIPLE

- Bring your *not enough* to Jesus.
- Invite his presence into whatever area needs a miracle.
- Celebrate every miracle in the midst of your hard places.

7

Living a Life
of Thank-You

Actually, the real game of Bigger and Better that Jesus
is playing with us usually isn't about money or posses-
sions or even our hopes. It's about our pride. He asks
if we'll give up that thing we're so proud of, that thing
we believe causes us to *matter* in the eyes of the world,
and give it up to follow Him.

Bob Goff, *Love Does: Discover a Secretly*
Incredible Life in an Ordinary World

The mirror revealed a woman in need of a shower, but I had
no time. I pulled my hair into a clippie and then ran through
the house, quickly cleaning all the parts that could be seen.
Do you know that feeling of stress? There's not enough time.

You're juggling ten different things and feel you aren't doing any of them well.

I don't know about you, but that's when irritation marches in, and I don't like the feeling. I climbed in my car and glanced at the clock.

The person who had volunteered to help with a meeting canceled last minute, which meant that all my well-laid plans weren't going to work. Which meant that I needed to leave a couple of hours early. Which meant that I didn't get a shower. Just writing these words makes me cringe. They feel whiney.

I'm not whiney.

Okay, on that day I was, and it had the power to impact not just my day but that of anyone I encountered.

Let's Get to Know Judas Iscariot

Jesus stands and wraps a towel around his waist. He kneels before each disciple and washes the grime from their dust-caked feet. It's a servant's task. One reserved for the lowest on the team.

"Very truly I tell you, one of you is going to betray me" (John 13:21).

His words are troubling. The men look around, confused. They have no clue who Jesus is talking about and stare at each other, at a loss (verse 22).

What does this tell us about Judas? There is nothing obvious in his character or interaction with the men around that table that indicates he has already betrayed Jesus for thirty pieces of silver. Not one person points to Judas and says, "I knew it! It's that guy. I've never trusted him." Instead, there is complete and total bewilderment. Judas is a nice guy, at least on the outside.

To you and me, that's incredible, because his reputation is that of the worst of sinners. His kiss pointed the soldiers to Jesus. He gave specific directions that allowed them to sneak up on Jesus in the dark and arrest him. He watched as they marched Jesus out of the garden to endure an unjust trial.

How does Judas feel as Jesus kneels to wash his dirty feet?

I have always imagined Judas Iscariot as a bad man. The reaction from his ministry partners and friends—those who lived side by side with him—reveals an entirely different picture. He was an ordinary man. He joked with them. They cared about each other. At one time he was trustworthy enough to be given the job of handling the money collected to meet their needs and those of the poor.

This isn't an evil villain in a movie or play. It's a man in whom Jesus saw worth and value, enough to draw him close to his side and in ministry. What in the world happened to Judas Iscariot, and what does his life teach us?

Come With Me

A Lack of Thank-You Festers in the Heart

It's the Passover celebration, and a crowd of powerful men have gathered to plot Jesus' death (Luke 22:1–3). Imagine their surprise when Judas steps boldly into their conversation and begins to negotiate for the betrayal of Jesus.

In Luke 22:3, three simple words are shared: *Satan entered Judas.* What a frightening thought! Is it possible that Judas Iscariot had no choice in the matter? Was he specifically chosen for this task to fulfill Scripture, as many have suggested? If so, it contradicts the purpose behind Jesus' life, death, and resurrection.

> For God did not send his Son into the world to condemn the
> world, but to save the world through him.
>
> John 3:17

The phrase *Satan entered Judas* is better interpreted this way:
The enemy put it into Judas's heart to betray Jesus. Judas was
tempted. The enemy knew Judas's weakness, just as he knows
ours. He is aware of what has been done in secret, for Judas
has been stealing from the treasury. Even as Judas witnessed
miracles, sat under anointed teaching, and ate with Jesus, he
dipped greedy fingers into coins earmarked to further the reach
of the gospel and meet the needs of the downtrodden. Along the
way he dropped clues like bread crumbs. Like the time Mary,
the sister of Martha, poured out perfume over Jesus' feet.

> "Why wasn't this perfume sold and the money given to the poor?
> It was worth a year's wages." [Judas] did not say this because
> he cared about the poor but because he was a thief; as keeper of
> the money bag, he used to help himself to what was put into it.
>
> John 12:5–6

Very few people, unless they are truly wicked, enter into a worthy cause only to end up embezzling. Somewhere along the way
his heart condition changed. That led to thievery and eventually
betrayal. The enemy knew his weakness and took full advantage.

> A good man brings good things out of the good stored up in his
> heart, and an evil man brings evil things out of the evil stored
> up in his heart. For the mouth speaks what the heart is full of.
>
> Luke 6:45

Judas had a choice. He could give in to the temptation or
take stock of his heart and deal with it. He continued down
a heartbreaking road. Let's look at John 12:6 one more time:

He did not say this because he cared about the poor but because he was a thief; as keeper of the money bag, he used to help himself to what was put into it.

He didn't start out as a thief. At one time he was intrigued by or cared enough about Jesus that he left everything to follow him. That's a huge sacrifice. As we study Judas's life, it might be easy to say, "I'd never give in to temptation on such a large scale!"

I'd never cheat on my husband.

I'd never steal money.

I'd never hurt anyone.

I'd never [fill in the blank with something you consider a big sin].

And you're right. There's a really great chance that, if given the opportunity to steal another woman's husband or take what is not ours, right up front we'd be aghast at the proposition. But the enemy is so much slyer than that. Temptation begins in the small things and burrows in to create discontent. We look around, and it seems like others have it better. We work hard. Why can't we have that too? That woman at work receives recognition when we deserve it more. Perhaps we see what another family or woman has—whether material things or success or children who don't throw fits in the grocery store—and we measure it against our life and it falls short. We begin to long for what we do not have. This is where the enemy strikes. It's where the stronghold begins. Discontentment sneaks in, we hold it close and feed it, and it spreads like cancer.

Judas wanted *more.*

Jesus hadn't tricked Judas. From the beginning he promised that things wouldn't always be easy (John 15:18–20). He often reminded the disciples (and us) that our rewards aren't luxury

125

or recognition (Luke 9:58). That day, as Judas stood in front of the corrupt men, he had the option to turn away from temptation. Someone would betray Jesus and fulfill the Scriptures, but it didn't have to be Judas. He walked away with enough money to buy a field and enough regrets to fill a lifetime.

That next evening, with the moon creeping between the tree limbs, Judas walks up to Jesus and kisses him. Jesus asks, "Judas, are you betraying the Son of Man with a kiss?" (Luke 22:48).

We rarely focus on this part of Judas's story. He runs back to the men in power and tries to give the blood money back. He begs them, but they refuse. This is where I mourn for all that Judas lost. He took his own life, not realizing that up until the last moment before he entered eternity, he still had an option. There is always room to turn back into the arms of Jesus. This same Jesus would later lean over and whisper to a criminal hanging on the cross beside him that his sins were forgiven.

Let's go back to that small room where Jesus stands with a towel wrapped around his waist. What might have happened if Judas had kissed Jesus on the cheek in gratitude, instead of in betrayal, in the garden of Gethsemane?

The same enemy that was aware of the discontent in Judas's heart is aware of the discontent in my own. The same enemy that tempted Judas tempts us.

How do we war against that enemy? We live a life of thank-you.

Living a life of thank-you thwarts the enemy in a thousand different encounters. He dares to stir up discontentment in our deepest relationships, and we find the good in the heart of that person. He tries to stir up discontentment in our ministry, and we find solutions for the problem instead. He tries to stir up discontentment in our faith, and we point to a bloodied cross and an open tomb.

He means to rob you, distract you, knock you down by slipping in a seed of ingratitude, and he cannot help but slink away when he finds a heart full of thank-you instead.

Intentional Gratitude

As I backed out of the garage that day, I felt the Holy Spirit tenderly pointing out my whiney self. I acknowledged the reality of my situation. Help would have been nice, but it wasn't available. There was more to consider. I began to whisper these words as I drove.

Thank you, Father, for this gorgeous day.

Thank you for last week when a friend let down her guard for the first time.

Thank you, Jesus, for leading Richard and me to this city.

Thank you that I can talk about this openly with you.

Thank you for our new friendships.

Thank you for that breath I just took.

I'm far from a saint. Those words weren't birthed out of feeling, but out of fact. They were real truths buried under my irritation. Believe me, I was tempted to give in and to make the problem bigger than it was. I was tempted to allow that to bleed into my attitude. I was tempted to let it shape the way I viewed everything about my day.

Discontentment leads us down a road God never intended us to travel.

I had caved enough to temptation, and I didn't like it much. It blinded me to the good all around me.

Intentional gratitude is a course corrector. It turns away temptation. You aren't asked to pretend that there aren't challenges, but to take a step back and tackle them in a different way.

Judas wasn't born so that he could die with a mountain of regrets. How do we recognize this ploy of the enemy? It often begins with unhappiness or dissatisfaction. Rather than addressing that need (which is a beautiful, strong response) in the presence of a God who loves us, we start looking at others or at things that we believe to be the source. *If I had what they have, things would be different.* This produces a harvest of discontentment.

How many ministries are destroyed as a lack of thank-you infiltrates?

How many marriages are damaged as a lack of thank-you wounds?

How many times do we forget what is priceless as we pursue or invest in things far less valuable? How many times are the innocent affected as our discontentment makes them feel as if they are responsible? In her book *Life Unstuck*, Pat Layton describes how we can regain our focus and live a life of gratitude.

> Unstuck praise requires us to focus on keeping our heart alarm engaged against intruders, and when we catch one, lock them up. You know what they look like, those pesky praise intruders:
> Disapproval and disrespect
> Complaints and criticism
> Impatience and whining
> Disregard and failure to appreciate
> Pessimism, bitterness, and discouragement.[1]

Living a life of thank-you takes a really close look at the intruders above. We're truthful with ourselves when we acknowledge they've become a part of our emotional DNA. Then we label them what they really are. They are thieves. They are temptations with the potential to harm, wound, damage, delay, and distract you.

My friend Nicki Koziarz, a busy working mom and author, says that when she feels this temptation, she asks herself a question: *What's it like to be on the other side of me?* She places herself in her children's shoes. A friend's personal space. The stranger on the other side of the counter. If she doesn't like what she sees, she acknowledges that she's battling temptation and stops so that she can tune her heart into Christ.

This is a question I've silently asked myself several times since she shared it. This isn't a weak position. You're not just battling discontentment; you're opening your heart to receive the gifts that you need to deal with the real issue. You're moving beyond your feelings to include the people within your personal space.

Live a Life of Thank-You Where You Are

Nearly thirty years ago I stood on the bottom rail of a rickety fence that wrapped around well over a hundred acres. Black Angus cattle chomped on grass in a nearby pasture. "This is going to be mine one day," the older guy said. He didn't plan to retire for years, but as the afternoon whiled away, he shared all of his dreams for "one day."

One day he was going to move back home, and this would all be his.

One day he'd do this or that with the cattle.

One day he'd fix that old house.

The problem was that none of it was his. The people who lived in it and owned it were very much alive. There was a chance that one day he'd inherit the old, white clapboard house and those rickety fences and that run-down tractor in the barn, but it wouldn't be anytime soon. He lived in a different state with his family, who preferred city life over the farm. He had a great job in the construction industry.

There's nothing wrong with dreaming. Many times those dreams are a catalyst to make a difference or to take a huge step of faith. Your dreams can encourage you when getting there is difficult. But this man's dreams were wrapped around something that wasn't his—which, when all was said and done, never became his.

> *Dreaming about tomorrow is worthwhile unless it makes you discontent with today.*

Dreaming is worthwhile unless it makes you unhappy with where you are or who you're with, or it creates resentment with God's timing versus your own. Dreaming is a gift unless it focuses on the fact that your neighbor's house is bigger than yours—in other words, what you don't have versus what you think you should have. In an ironic twist, my farm-dreaming friend passed away before the last of his elderly relatives did. I often wondered how much he missed, plotting and thinking and worrying about that acreage and worn-down house, while failing to appreciate what he had right in front of him.

Should we dream big? Absolutely. Should we obsess, worry, wrangle, or plot to get what we want, or to have what someone else has? Probably not the best plan.

I once overheard someone say, "If you can write a check for it, it's not priceless."

Living a life of thank-you shifts our definition of *priceless* from those things that carry a price tag (a title, a dollar amount, a thing, a feeling, something we really, really want) to the things we already have that are irreplaceable.

That child in the other room? The one in his Wreck-It Ralph stage of toddlerhood with sweet kisses and potty training?

Priceless.

That man who's gaining a few pounds and who loves you when you wake up with halitosis and bedhead hair?

Priceless.

That friend who stands beside you even when you're wearing your cranky pants?

Priceless.

A Savior who came to serve and wash my dirty feet?

Priceless, priceless, priceless.

When You're Not Naturally Grateful

Living a life of thank-you might not come naturally to you. For some, the normal exit is toward negativity. Should you even try? Yes, and here's the promise: The more you practice it, the more ingrained it becomes. There's a new groove formed in your thinking, and the more you gravitate toward it, the deeper and more natural it becomes. You're still your same old funny, snarky self (or however God made you), but gratitude threads throughout. In his book *I Like Giving*, Brad Formsma says:

> There's something incredible about giving when it's our idea. Opening our eyes and ears to the people around us and asking, "How can we give?" is a profoundly life-giving and satisfying way to live. One of Jesus' ideas was that it was more blessed to give than to receive. I have found that to be true.[2]

Give less to the perishable and more to the priceless.

Can I share something? It's a lot easier to complain or stay in a rut than it is to step outside your immediate feelings or long-nurtured negative attitude and offer up gratitude. But gratitude is one of the most profound and easiest ways to give. That's why we verbalize the blessings, not just on a busy day when we're juggling and nothing's going right, but when the stakes are higher. Saying the words out loud is your kiss on Jesus' cheek.

Let's pause and do it together:

Thank you for that meal.

Thank you for our home that shelters me and those I love.

Thank you that I call out your name and you hear me.

Now list at least five more things for which *you* are thankful. It not only changes the flight path of your attitude, but helps you discover hidden blessings.

My mother is seventy-seven. When I come to visit her and it's the least bit chilly outside, she asks me to wear a coat. I usually grin and tease her, reminding her that I know when I'm warm or cold. But my thoughts could go down this path instead: *I don't want to wear a coat just so that you can feel warmer. If I wanted to wear a coat, I would have brought one. . . .* Do you see where these thoughts can take us? Intentional gratitude reminds me of these things:

Thank you, Lord, that my mom cares about my well-being.

Thank you that she thinks of me.

Thank you that I have my mom.

Thank you that I can visit her, for I know one day I'll look back and see these moments as treasures.

So I grab a coat and toss it around my shoulders. I kiss her on her cheek and hold her close. Why would I get my heart in a wad over something so small? I'm treasuring my mom instead. I'm thankful that she cares about my well-being. Living a life of thank-you has the power to completely change your relationships. Consider how simple words of gratitude might feel on a crammed, stressful day. We love to receive them. Living a life of thank-you changes how we feel inside, how we view life, and the lasting mark we leave on others. This isn't about being fake, but purposeful. It's being brave enough to look in the mirror and ask hard questions. It's holding up the answers to God and asking him to change us in the areas that need his touch.

Am I consistently negative, or purposefully thankful?

Am I so caught up in what I want tomorrow that I've forgotten how precious today can be?

Has discontentment directed me down a road God never intended?

Am I taking for granted the priceless treasures right in front of me?

What is the root of my dissatisfaction?

How do I deal with it in a healthy way?

What does the enemy desire to steal from me through discontentment?

For a moment let's join the disciples around the table. Notice that Jesus has just wrapped a towel around his waist. See him kneeling at your feet, tenderly washing the grime and discontent away.

Let your kiss be one of gratitude.

Let your words follow. Put on a heart of thank-you until it becomes who you are.

Taking It Deeper

1. Is ingratitude a sin? Why or why not?

2. Describe the difference between a healthy desire for something and an unhealthy desire. At what point does it cross from healthy to unhealthy?

3. Read Philippians 4:11–13. In what ways is it possible for a naturally negative or ungrateful attitude to change?

4. If you were to live a life of thank-you in your closest relationships, what might that look like? (Get down to the nitty-gritty, the small things. How will you practice this for the next few days?)

5. Why were the disciples unaware of Judas's heart condition? How easy is it for discontentment to be hidden, yet doing an ugly work inside?

6. To the very end there was an opportunity for redemption for Judas. What does his example teach us?

7. Choose for one day to live a life of thank-you. Come back twenty-four hours later. How difficult was it? Did it come naturally? Describe one response (yours or another person's) that resulted.

8. Read John 13:8–9. At first Peter resisted Jesus' washing his feet, but then he wanted everything he had to offer. How did this show gratitude toward Jesus? What does it teach us?

SCRIPTURE

Peter said to Him, "Never shall You wash my feet!" Jesus answered him, "If I do not wash you, you have no part with Me." Simon Peter said to Him, "Lord, then wash not only my feet, but also my hands and my head."

John 13:8–9 NASB

PRAYER

Father, I'm blessed. Today I count those blessings, and I am grateful for each. Help me to live a life of thank-you. Let gratitude become a part of me.

LIVING AS A DISCIPLE

- Count the cost of ingratitude.
- Prioritize what is priceless in your life.
- When you sense discontentment creeping in, counter it with gratitude.
- As a kiss of gratitude, do one selfless thing for someone today.

8

When You Feel Like the Chair Guy

If you are marked by God, you don't need to be marketed by man.

Christine Caine

"I wonder if I'll get to heaven one day and hear God say, 'Hey, that's the guy who set up chairs.'"

After a week of ministering to youth and taking calls from parents—who may or may not have been happy with him at any given time—my friend vented while unfolding the metal chairs and pushing them into a straight line. It was one of many behind-the-scenes routine tasks he performed week after week, none of which were taught in Bible school.

Then there's my friend Lynn and her husband, Greg. They wake up at 5:00 a.m. every Sunday and drive to church, where they unload sound equipment and set up hundreds of chairs. They drive home afterward, shower, and then drive back to church to worship. They've done this for years.

Recently I spoke at two services in my own church on Mother's Day. Rather than a traditional building, we meet in a local Boys and Girls Club. When I arrived early for the first service, I was greeted by a team sweating in the early-morning hours as they hauled out chairs. I spoke in the second service as well. As soon as the building cleared, a second team moved from their spots and started to stack chairs onto a moving trailer, break down equipment, and sweep the floors.

I held a microphone in my hands that day. It was a privilege to share the gospel with nearly two thousand people—all of whom sat in chairs placed by mostly unseen hands.

Every Sunday across the world, someone is setting up chairs. All to draw people to Jesus.

What does it mean to be the chair guy spiritually? It's not a role most of us seek willingly, but it's foundational to our faith.

Let's Say Hello to Andrew

When we hear about the inner circle, three are almost exclusively mentioned—Peter, James, and John. Andrew is also a part of that inner circle. Yet Andrew is listed last, or not at all. He's there, but he's not front and center.

Simon Peter is his older brother. I'm a middle child myself, so I know what it's like to try to find my spot in a crowd of siblings. In Andrew's culture, his ranking is decided for him. It is customary for the firstborn son to have ultimate authority over younger siblings. They get first rights. The greater share of the inheritance. To be the boss of the younger siblings.

Is Andrew less important than Peter, James, or John? If seeing one's name on the roster is an indicator, some might say he's last, perhaps even least. We might wonder if Andrew is missing the "it" factor.

Only, he's *first* to recognize Jesus as Messiah.

Andrew is a disciple of John the Baptist. Andrew has listened as John teaches about the long-awaited Messiah. One day Jesus walks by. He's been in a forty-day battle in the wilderness. He's hungry and weak in body, but his face shines with the Spirit of God. John leaps to his feet and calls out, "Look! There is the lamb of God!" (John 1:36 NLT).

Andrew stands to peer at the haggard man walking past him. He grabs a friend and follows Jesus down the road.

Jesus turns and asks, "What do you want?"

"Where are you staying?" Andrew says.

"Come and see."

Andrew remains in the presence of Jesus the rest of the day. When he finally leaves, he runs to find his brother, Simon. Can you picture this scene? He grabs his older brother by the arms and sings out the good news. "We've found the Messiah!"

Andrew is so certain that Jesus is the Savior that he convinces his older brother to meet him. When they stand face-to-face, Jesus looks intently into the eyes of Simon Peter and says the strangest thing:

"You are now the Rock (Cephas)."

What a powerful moment for Simon Peter. But let's step into Andrew's sandals for a moment. Do you know that feeling when a person grabbed from the back row is placed on center stage for the solo, while someone hands you the props to put in the storage closet? That's what just took place with Andrew.

He was the *first* to believe.

He was the *first* to tell someone the good news.

If this were a race, he'd earn a medal. It wouldn't go to the guy who had to be dragged to the starting line.

Come With Me

Unseen and Unimportant Aren't the Same Thing

Maybe you understand how Andrew feels. You have been faithful. You work hard. You're doing all the right things, but it feels like everyone else is noticed. God seems to be promoting others to the front of the class while you're still faithfully turning in your homework and showing up for every class.

You have dreams too.

You're working hard in that area too.

Andrew discovered something about being first that has the potential to change us. It's the biblical definition of success. If we figure it out and start living like it's true, we stop looking at other people to determine whether we're first or last.

Andrew became renowned as Saint Andrew after he ministered, bridging the gap between the Greek people and the gospel. His role was to bring people to Jesus, and he did that well. He led his brother to Jesus. He brought the boy with the fishes (John 6:8) to Jesus when the hungry crowd didn't have enough to eat. When a crowd of Greek men told Andrew and Philip that they wanted to know more about Jesus, Andrew inquired on their behalf (John 12:20–22) so that the answers might change their lives forever.

His faithfulness to bring people to Jesus impacted generations.

What allows you to impact eternity?

That's how we define success as followers of Christ. That might be holding a microphone or a baby in the nursery. That might be stacking chairs, or stacking dollars because you're trust-worthy with a ministry's money. Success is kneeling in front of a neglected child and inviting him or her to dinner. It's opening your home to tweens who are loud and make messes and eat you out of house and home, yet who feel loved in your home. It's staying in a job that you love because it's impacting people, but it's not going to propel you to the executive suite. Success is fighting spiritually for your closest relationships and watching kernels of hope spring out of your prayers. It's holding close to your faith when your child goes the opposite direction of what he's been taught, and you find peace in God's promises.

> *Success is not about a specific feat, but about finding where you fit.*

Success might be encouraging someone else in their giftings while you remain out of the limelight. Success is what takes place when no one is looking and you're studying and preparing and practicing, all because one person might be introduced to Jesus.

Success is waking up and seeking him before you run straight into your day.

We are all the chair guys. Every last one of us. We are least. We are last. We are first. We are seen. We are unseen. We are working together with one purpose.

But can we be honest with each other? Sometimes stacking chairs isn't where we want to be. We want to zip past the chair stacking to the payoff. The feel-good stuff. The tangible ding-ding-ding that says we just won our reward.

Christine Caine, in her book *Unstoppable*, says that people often tell her that they wish they could follow in her footsteps.

Thank you for being my safe place to mourn my dream. But more so, thank you for reminding me that I did it for you, and you found pleasure in it.

—Suzie

They want to make a big impact. Or stand on a stage and speak to thousands. She explains to them that she didn't arrive on a worldwide stage without her "darkroom" experience. She has mopped up vomit after silly food-game mishaps when she served as a youth leader. (I've been there. Have you?) As an A21 founder, she has sat with her heart pounding, waiting to receive the phone call that says one more girl has been rescued from sex trafficking. The darkroom experience is where she's unseen by the world. It's where God sees her motivations for ministry, and she keeps going because she wants to be exactly where he has her at the moment.[1]

Every part of our experience counts. The call on our hearts. The darkroom experiences. The moments when the light is on us. When the lights go out.

Christine reminds us that "Destiny is not an instant click and upload."[2] Instead, in those places where you are unseen, but where you know you hear the voice of God and you keep going, that's where God develops you. It's where the word *success* transitions to *call*, where you long to hear the voice of God over worrying about your reward. It's where you are free to dream big—but you consider all the parts along the way just as important as the final destination.

Sure, we all want to be acknowledged. We want someone to notice that we've been faithful. He does.

> Whatever you do, work at it with all your heart, as working for the Lord, not for human masters, since you know that you will receive an inheritance from the Lord as a reward. It is the Lord Christ you are serving.
>
> Colossians 3:23–24

God doesn't look at credits to determine success. We don't have to be tangled in the pressures of society, or even of our Christian culture. In fact, we can begin to celebrate the fact that we're the chair guy.

Can I tell you something? Right now I'm sitting in my living room with my laptop. I'm wearing yoga pants and a faded T-shirt. My toenails are red-chipped. I wouldn't want any of you to see my messy ponytail and no-makeup face (okay, I wouldn't mind too much). My sweet guy is sitting across from me writing therapy notes for the little ones of tender age who need counseling because of abuse or neglect or for whom life has been hard. This afternoon we ran for a moment to spend time with our daughter, Melissa. We brought lunch and then played Hungry Hippo for a few minutes with Josiah and Luke so she could have a few minutes to herself.

All of these are chair-guy moments. Unseen, at least by the majority of the world, but they count. The little things. The big. The ones that have the label of ministry, and those that really are ministry, just without the label.

> Serve wholeheartedly, as if you were serving the Lord, not people.
>
> Ephesians 6:7

If excellence is defined as working at it with all of your heart, as if you were personally doing it for Jesus, then bring it on.

Being the chair guy means exchanging our cultural definition of success to discover what really matters.

If loving those babies and helping them grow into strong, faith-filled adults is where you are, celebrate that.

If it's behind the scenes where no one sees you, but it brings people to him, let's delight in being a part of building his church.

We can build a large bank account or impressive byline or get our names on the brochure with our own human efforts, and there's satisfaction to be found in those things. But doing them as if working for the Lord means that the bank account, that byline, or that name in print doesn't identify you. If you lose it or it doesn't work out like you thought it should, you've not lost your sense of worth or value. You're doing it for him. And if it's greater than you ever thought possible, you ask God what he wants to do with it. Then you just keep doing what brings you joy, living in your sweet spot as you bring people to Christ in whatever you do.

What Do We Do With Disappointment?

Fifteen years ago I wrote my first book. It was a book for teens. I was beyond excited when I signed the contract. I made a notebook and put a color copy of the cover on the front. On my calendar I circled the day the book would be released to the public.

My publisher told me about a trade show that would be held in Denver, Colorado. All of the new books from various Christian publishers would be launched to distributors and bookstores at this convention. They said I should come and hold a book signing at their booth. It was a sacrifice for my family to pay out of pocket, because my advance for working on the book for nine months corresponded to my status as a brand-new author—it was really, really small. But I was determined to make it work!

When I arrived, I stood in the convention center in awe. I glanced down at my ID tag, which labeled me as "Author," and sighed in happiness. Somewhere in that room the size of two football fields was my book, and I went in search. I finally reached the spot where my publisher's booth was supposed to be and was greeted with a surprise. A large portable gray wall stood where the booth should have been. A sign on it said SOLD. My publisher had been acquired by another company a couple of days before the trade show. It had happened quickly, so this announcement that greeted me and the others who traveled to sign our books was how we learned the news. Instead of a fancy booth with books and editors and long lines of potential readers, my book cover (with no pages) was hanging on the wall like a child's art display at the mall.

I had walked into that convention center with my dreams held close. With one swoop, they fell into a heap. My hotel room was prepaid for three days. Changing my ticket would cost even more. For three long days I wandered the aisles, silently watching lines of eager readers and the authors who signed their books for them. I stood in line to get my free books. I piled the free books in my carry-on.

At least I'll salvage something from the trip.

I left questioning whether I was supposed to be a writer. I wondered if I should go back to a job I didn't like very much, but which rewarded me with tangible success markers like a regular paycheck and a name on the door rather than the inconsistency of publishing. I'd had a definition of success engraved in my brain from an early age: hard work + due diligence = victory.

Then why was hard work + due diligence adding up to disappointment instead? I tried to put on the best face and be happy for friends whose book was in their hands, but I was jealous.

I've learned a lot since then. I've written several books and thousands of articles. But I've transitioned my focus from how many books I might sell or how cool it is to have my byline in a magazine or on a book cover to the reader who will hold it in her hands. I wish I could say that this paradigm shift in my thinking came overnight, but it didn't. My disappointments held the power to make me bitter or better.

If our definition of success is solely based on outcome, we'll live like we're on a never-ending bungee jump. We're up. We're down. We're swayed by failure or buoyed by success. We're left hanging until someone reels us in with a word of praise.

When all he asks us to do is our best.

Fast-forward fifteen years. My seventh book had just been released. Two months later I received a letter. My publisher had been bought by a larger publisher. They were uncertain of what would happen to all inventory, including my book, which had been on the shelves for only a few weeks.

I sat on my living room floor with the letter in my hands, numb. It seemed against all odds, but the reality was that three out of the seven books I had written were impacted by publisher sales, reorganizations, or decisions beyond my control.

I'm not going to lie. Disappointment doesn't feel any less painful on the seventh book than it does on the first. There wasn't one thing I could do about it—except trust. I worked hard. I prayed over that book. There were months of tears and study and joy poured into it. Sixteen years ago Jesus said the words "Come with me, Suzie," and that led to writing words about him. He didn't promise me fame or an easy path. He just asked me to bring people to him, in the best way I knew how. Lysa TerKeurst, in *The Best Yes*, says:

> In the midst of the unexpected, we have an opportunity to make one of our greatest Best Yes decisions ever. Let this unexpected happening point to your strength, not your weakness. Maybe you've been entrusted with this. Not cursed with it.[3]

Later that week I received an email from a woman named Claudia. She sent an image of herself sitting on the bed. The bedspread was red and yellow floral, and on it rested her Bible and my book. Yellow sticky notes with handwritten words lay all around her feet. Claudia had lost her husband to cancer. It came fast and he left earth quickly. She was now a single mom, widowed and heartbroken, and she shared these words with me: "I didn't think I'd ever heal, but your book is helping me find the way."

Lord, I get it. Thank you. I finally got it. This is not about me.

As I wrote that book in a small prayer room in Fayetteville, God and I had worshiped together. Every time I put my fingers on the keyboard, just as I am doing now, I prayed for the woman who would one day read it. There were times that I stood with my hands uplifted, overwhelmed at his Word and the gentleness in which it is revealed in the lives of those who receive it. Whether my book made it into one million hands or into the hands of Claudia, I had been entrusted with a task.

I did my part. The book was written with one purpose—to draw the broken to the Healer. If Claudia was the one he had on his heart when I wrote it, then it was enough.

A few months ago I received another email. It told me that my book *The Mended Heart: God's Healing for Your Broken Places* was going to be used as the primary book for an international ministry as their summer online Bible study.

The book was released from the depths of a warehouse and brought back to life.

Just as I had no control over my third publisher buyout, I had no control over this exciting new development. I was in awe as thousands of women signed up to read the study—women from all over the world.

From every state in the U.S.

From Africa. Australia. India. Bangladesh. New Zealand. And beyond. I giggled when the ministry asked me to sign two thousand books for the first wave of readers. Do you know how many two thousand books is? It's a pallet of forty-plus cases. I signed until my hand cramped. Day after day. The employees at the distribution warehouse sauntered by. "You okay there?" they'd ask. I wasn't just okay. I was ecstatic. Sure, my wrist hurt so badly that I soaked it in Epsom salts at night, but every time I signed a book I thought of Claudia.

Lord, let this one go into the hands of someone like her. A woman seeking you.

> Be dressed ready for service and keep your lamps burning, like servants waiting for their master to return from a wedding banquet, so that when he comes and knocks they can immediately open the door for him. It will be good for those servants whose master finds them watching when he comes. Truly I tell you, he will dress himself to serve, will have them recline at the table and will come and wait on them. It will be good for those servants whose master finds them ready, even if he comes in the middle of the night or toward daybreak.
>
> Luke 12:35–38

If I had found "success" without my disappointments, I'm not certain that I would have experienced the joy of working for the One. I'm not sure that Claudia would have been my focus. It might have sat squarely on me.

What is success?

It's setting up the chairs. No matter what that looks like. Front row. Limelight. Out of sight. We're bringing people to Jesus, and that's worth dancing over!

What About Andrew?

In the end Andrew was martyred, hung on an X-shaped cross. He told the authorities that he couldn't bear to be crucified in the same manner as Jesus. Even in death he honored his Messiah. The chair guy made an eternal impact all the way to the very end.

TAKING IT DEEPER

1. Quickly throw out five words that describe success.

2. How does a scriptural definition of success conflict with any of those words?

3. Read Luke 18:18–23. Was Jesus' answer too harsh? Why or why not?

4. Quickly throw out five words that describe failure. How does the scriptural definition of success conflict with any of these words?

5. Describe a time you resented being the chair guy. Has your perception of that season changed?

6. Is there anything wrong with being successful? Explain your answer.

7. Read Luke 16:10–11. What is expected with what we've been given (whether finances, power, prestige, honor, success, fame, behind-the-scenes service, loved ones, etc.)?

SCRIPTURE

Each of you should use whatever gift you have received to serve others, as faithful stewards of God's grace in its various forms.

1 Peter 4:10

PRAYER

Lord, redefine success from what I have or what I become or how much I earn to bringing people to you. Let those I love see you in me. Let my unseen life bring you just as much joy as that which is seen by people. What a gift it is to bring people to you.

LIVING AS A DISCIPLE

- Whatever you are doing, do it as if it's for him.
- Shift the focus from results to people.
- Count the unseen as important as the "seen."
- Celebrate the eternal impact of what you do (no matter what that is).

9

The Fallacy of a Storm-Free Life

Peace isn't a byproduct of control, the payout of a happy conclusion. Peace is the infiltrating, life-giving presence of a very real God. One who loves nothing more than to step into the middle of locked and darkened rooms and impossible circumstances, close enough to touch.

Michele Cushatt, *Undone*

Sometimes we lie to people who are new to faith. Our heart is in the right place as we say something like, "Just kneel or say these words after me, and your life will be wonderful." They kneel and repeat the prayer, and they do feel better, so it must be true. Then they go home and slap right into the wall of real life.

Loved ones don't understand their faith in Jesus. The battle that raged yesterday is still brewing. Unexpected circumstances blow up and they wonder, *Aren't things supposed to be wonderful?*

Maybe we could tell them this instead:

Following Jesus isn't a charmed life; it's a changed life.

As a young teen, I left the small Tulsa, Oklahoma, church feeling something I didn't know existed moments before. I had encountered Jesus! I believed in him, at least to the best of my ability. I look back today and see a girl who had no religious bones in her body. That next weekend I tried to explain my faith to friends, who didn't get it. That very same weekend temptation crept in—and I didn't even know what temptation was. I was falling in love with my Savior, but I also felt the pull of sin. I caved in that night, and walked home afterward, weeping.

Before, I wouldn't have given it a thought, but somehow my encounter with Jesus had already begun to teach me that sin grieved him . . . because I mattered to him. My sorrow included not just my sin, but the fact that every last person I had told about Jesus witnessed that failure. It was a storm of my own making, born out of feelings and immaturity and a choice I wish I hadn't made.

Then there are those storms that have nothing to do with your choices. You pray at your bedside each night. You read your Bible, and you understand the love of Christ. You recognize temptation, and though you will never claim to be perfect, your desire is to honor him with your life. And yet you are in a storm. You didn't see it coming. It's raging and you want out. You've listened to thousands of sermons and read Scripture.

You've heard that if you tithe, you receive a return. Yet you've lost your job, and the light bill and mortgage are due.

You've heard that God is the Healer, but you struggle with sickness that won't go away, and you're tired of being sick.

These types of storms have many faces. Financial struggles. Sickness or disease. Maybe the man you love walks away from his vows or out of your life. Or that move across country leaves you feeling alone.

My first storm as a believer knocked me off my feet. But I confessed my sin, and mercy picked me up and soothed me, and told me that tomorrow was another day. Forty years later, it's the storms that blow up out of nowhere that can feel the most unsettling. When these storms take place, especially if we've been promised or believe in a storm-free life, it might leave us wondering, *Where are you, God?*

Let's Sit in the Boat With Judas (Not Iscariot)

Where are you, God? That's the question asked one stormy day by Judas and the other disciples.

> One day Jesus said to his disciples, "Let us go over to the other side of the lake." So they got into a boat and set out. As they sailed, he fell asleep. A squall came down on the lake, so that the boat was being swamped, and they were in great danger.
>
> Luke 8:22–23

Jesus is at the height of his popularity, and throngs of people—sometimes thousands—flock to him wherever he goes. They bring their sick, and many are healed, which only creates greater crowds. More come. They sit in the blazing sun to hear his teaching. Just a few days earlier, his mother and brothers stood outside the door asking him to pause his work and to spend time with his family. He was in ministry mode. Pursuing the Father's will. He turned them down.

Jesus is exhausted, so he takes an unplanned break. "Let's go to the other shore, guys."

He boards the rugged seacraft, then curls up on the hard floor of the vessel and falls asleep. He's surrounded by ropes and fishing spears and netting, all covered by the odor of fish, and yet he slumbers on. He has poured out, and now his human side begs him to fill back up.

Sudden squalls are not uncommon in that broken, torn terrain. Clouds dance and grow dark with rain. The storm races down violent and raging, so quickly that they are unprepared. The boat takes on water, even as the more seasoned fishermen wrestle to keep the boat from sinking. They shout Jesus' name.

> The disciples went and woke him, saying, "Master, Master, we're going to drown!" He got up and rebuked the wind and the raging waters; the storm subsided, and all was calm. "Where is your faith?" he asked his disciples. In fear and amazement they asked one another, "Who is this? He commands even the winds and the water, and they obey him."
>
> Luke 8:24–25

A few years ago I was in Perrault Falls, Canada, visiting relatives. They owned a small home nestled near a large lake. One sultry afternoon we swatted big black flies on our trek to reach the boat tethered to shore. Within minutes we were in the middle of the lake. I couldn't wait to catch my limit of walleye. Nearly an hour later, we had explored several of the fishing spots recommended by our hosts. We were a long way from our original launch site when a squall brewed out of nowhere. One moment the clouds were floating, and the next they gathered, darkened and swirling, right above our heads. Water sloshed into the small boat. We pulled our fishing gear in and started back. The water that had been crystal clear moments before was choppy and frothing and beat against the boat. The temperature dropped ten degrees in a matter of seconds. I shivered as I grabbed my life jacket and put it on. The thought that we might capsize felt very real. There's no more heartfelt prayer sent up to heaven than when you think you might be about to enter its gates.

Visibility was near zero. Rain lashed. Waves threw us up and down as we tried to figure out how to get to shore. Any shore. The engine stalled and we grabbed the oars. The rain broke just enough to see a small island in the near distance, and we rowed until it felt like our arms would break. The engine finally restarted, and we found shelter.

When I try to tell this story to friends who've never been caught in a squall, they dismiss it. "It's a lake. How dangerous could it be?"

Our hosts assured us that we were lucky. They know what can happen when visibility is zero, when you've lost your sense of direction, and when your boat fills with water and you can't bail it out quickly enough. Just as we had prayed in our boat that stormy afternoon, the disciples feared for their lives and called on Jesus. "Master, Master, we're going to drown!" In Matthew's gospel these words are added: "Save us, Lord, or we perish!" (see 8:25).

Let's sit in that boat for a moment and watch Judas as the storm rages.

His name is recorded a few different ways in Scripture. He's called Jude, but not Jude the brother of Jesus. He's called Judas, but not Judas Iscariot. Sometimes he's referred to by the nickname of Thaddeus. Most scholars agree that he's not the author of the book of Jude in the Bible. He's only mentioned twice in the New Testament, so what we know about Judas is mostly who he's *not*.

There's one more "not" about Judas.

He's not a fisherman. He's a farmer by trade. If the fishermen—like Peter and James and John, who grew up living and breathing the ancient art of fishing—are terrified, how does Judas feel?

Scared.

Terrified.

Perhaps he just wants Jesus to wake up and do *something*.

Do you relate? That's what we might feel when we're thrust into a storm for which we feel ill-equipped.

Come With Me

If Jesus Is in the Boat, You're in Good Company

Jesus wakes up to faces crowded around him. "Master, Master. Wake up!"

He stands. The boat sways and tumbles over the waves. Nearby, disciples furiously try to empty the boat of water. "Be still!" he says.

Then, as if the storm had never happened, the waters are still and smooth as silk. Skies clear. Flapping sails settle. Jesus turns to them. "Where is your faith?"

I don't know what your response would be, but I've been in unexpected storms—like sickness and medical expenses—that felt like they were taking us under. In these seasons I'm praying, and it's all I can do to hang on. In those times I may have responded to Jesus' question with any of the following:

I was calling your name, Jesus, and I didn't know if you heard me.

I woke up and got out of bed today, and that took all the faith I had.

155

I know you're near, but my faith feels a million miles away.
I am holding on to truth, though the circumstances say I am going under. I'm afraid, Jesus. Do you see what's going on?

Was Jesus requesting a specific answer from the disciples? It doesn't appear so. He just wanted them to be still. His words calmed the heavens, but his powerful words had just as much authority to calm the fears of the men clinging to the sides of the boat. They had done all they knew to do. The storm was bigger than they were.

Be still, Judas. Be still, Peter. Be still, Bartholomew.
Be still, Suzie.
Be still, [your name here].

Jesus had told them they were going to the other side of the lake. They were safe all along. If Jesus was in the boat with them, they would not go under.

A friend and his wife found out that she had cancer, and it was aggressive. That next Sunday he stepped onto the platform of his church and sang the classic "The Anchor Holds" by Ray Boltz. Tears covered his cheeks as he started the chorus, "The anchor holds though the ship's been battered."[1]

This young father and husband had no idea what the future held. He was in a storm, but he trusted that Jesus was in the boat with him. The longer I live, the more opportunities I have to be on the front row as men and women of faith get hit by unexpected circumstances, myself included. Sometimes I've witnessed miracles of healing, marriages restored, a son or daughter freed from addiction. Other times I've watched as believers made it to the other shore battered and windswept. Their situation hadn't changed, but they were anchored as they clung to their faith, because nothing holds quite so strongly.

We can be *still* in a storm.

This isn't a false promise, like "When you become a believer, everything is going to be wonderful." It's a rich truth that says we are not alone in the midst of trials. If you are in a storm right now, be still. Take a breath. Inhale the promise that he's in the boat with you.

Reaching the Shore

None of us want to be in a storm, not willingly. It makes us afraid. We aren't sure that it will end. We don't know what to do when it rages long past what we hoped.

I've been there. I know what it is to walk around my house seven times praying for God to provide for my family when, despite working as hard as we can, there's not enough income to meet basic needs. I know what it is to feel your world topple with not one but two diagnoses of cancer. I know what it feels like to crawl into bed and pull my covers over my head and say, "God, I have no clue what to do," in a situation with a loved one.

Sometimes the greatest surprises come in our greatest trials.

Yet it is in the storm that you discover who he is and, in the process, a whole lot more about *you*.

> Pure gold put in the fire comes out of it proved pure; genuine faith put through this suffering comes out proved genuine. When Jesus wraps this all up, it's your faith, not your gold, that God will have on display as evidence of his victory.
>
> 1 Peter 1:7 The Message

Storms happen. He's not unaware that you're in one. That storm isn't the end of your story, but another chapter stamped on your faith. You were battered. You were water-soaked. You called out his name. You found courage, strength, and endurance that you didn't know existed within you.

I shared with you that Richard was diagnosed with cancer while I walked this journey. We also lost a beautiful grand-baby-to-be as I took this journey. We knew her name. We had already fallen in love with this sweet little girl. I won't share much about this loss, because as a family we're still fresh in the grief of that loss. Our faith is a safe place to mourn. I know that when we pray for our beautiful children who lost this precious little girl, God hears those prayers and brings them comfort.

When our world collapses beneath us, we are not without strength. We are not swept away, forever lost. We are anchored by our faith in him. We are held close in those storms.

> The Lord is my strength and my shield; my heart trusts in him, and he helps me. My heart leaps for joy, and with my song I praise him.
>
> Psalm 28:7

We are anchored by his Word.

We are anchored by his presence.

We are anchored by peace that makes no sense in relation to our circumstances.

We are also anchored by the incredible strength we find through each other. Praying for one another. Loving one another. Lifting one another up. And incredibly, though our hearts may be heavy, our spirits can be light.

Your Faith Will Not Be Shipwrecked

> "Who can this be? For He commands even the winds and water, and they obey Him!"
>
> Luke 8:25 NKJV

Judas and the disciples had observed multiple miracles, but this? Jesus *rebuked* the winds. He didn't look up at the skies and say, "Hey, this is a really big storm." He rose up in authority against it. God the Father is the Creator of the sky and winds, but Jesus' words were not for him.

Rather, he was rising up against one who dared to stir fear in the hearts of his disciples. For the past several days Jesus had been teaching his disciples. Not long before they boarded the boat, Jesus taught them the story of the seed (Luke 8:5–15). Some of the seed fell on shallow soil, and birds ate it. Other seed fell on rocky soil, and the seedlings died from lack of moisture. Some seed fell on thorny soil, and was choked by thorns. Then there was the seed that fell on good soil, and it yielded a crop that was a hundred times more than what was sown.

Jesus planted the Word in the hearts and minds of thousands.

Some listened, but then something or someone swooped in and stole their enthusiasm—but not the disciples.

Others received the Word, but when hard times came they called it a day—but not the disciples.

Some allowed weeds to choke out their faith—but not these men!

The men in the boat were good soil. Jesus had planted his Word in them. The disciples didn't always understand, but they followed Jesus. They didn't shy away when the Word exposed shallow soil or rocky places that needed tending. They were far from perfect, but there was rich soil in each of their hearts.

Jesus *rebuked* the winds because the enemy thought he could use the storm to shipwreck these men's faith. Jesus declared to the enemy that the seed planted in their hearts would withstand the storm. After he addressed the enemy, Jesus pushed the seed a little deeper into the disciples' hearts.

"Teacher, don't you care if we drown?" (Mark 4:38).

The Greek word translated as "drown" is *apollymi*, which means "all is lost."

Don't you care if we *drown?*

"We" isn't just the disciples. They are a team. They are all in the boat. This includes Jesus. Sometimes you read something in Scripture, and though you've read it a hundred times, you see it for the first time. The disciples are talking about more than a boat sinking. If the boat capsizes, they'll lose all they have been building together for the kingdom. The object of their faith is slumbering on the floor of the boat.

Good soil, good soil, good soil!

Certainly, there's fear. But these men so loved Jesus and the work they were doing together that they feared all would be lost. He had told them they were going to the other side. He was in the boat with them.

Sometimes our greatest fear is that our faith will be shipwrecked in the midst of sickness or financial battles or when loved ones are thrust into chaos. Luke 8:15 assures us, "But the seed on good soil stands for those with a noble and good heart, who hear the word, retain it, and by persevering produce a crop."

He's *in* you. You are good soil. He rebukes the winds and storms for you, but his assurance is that there's something on the other side of the storm. Renewed faith. Hope. Strength gained from grabbing his hand in the storm.

His Word in the Storm

In Oklahoma, most people are not afraid of sirens or tornado warnings. Some might climb into a bathtub or head to a shelter, but most stand on the porch taking pictures.

But if you see the hook developing, that's a different story. It's time to take cover.

Years ago, Richard and I lived on a farm in an eleven-hundred-square-foot wood-siding house. The windows let in frigid air in the winter and blistering heat in the summer. If a tornado were to hit that house, we'd have landed somewhere in Kansas, because it didn't have the bones to withstand an F3 tornado. During one storm when the sirens went off, I waited outside, ready to go to the shelter. In the distance the shelf cloud was black and ominous. There were tiny hooks dancing up and down at the bottom of the clouds.

"Richard, come on!" I shouted.

He appeared at the back door, arms filled. He had a jar of peanut butter, a loaf of bread, and other food items. No flashlight. No blankets. Nothing that would allow us to tune in to the outside world. But we had the fixings for a peanut butter sandwich.

We all respond differently in a storm.

Some run for cover. Some settle in on the front porch and watch. Some take pictures and post them to Instagram. Some chase the storm. Some worry until the last cloud floats away. Some grab a jar of peanut butter. Regardless of how we respond in a weather-related emergency, we can prepare for unexpected trials or hard places.

Somewhere in my first few months of living in the book of Luke, I stumbled upon a video taken of persecuted Christians. They had memorized large chunks of Scripture and shared it in secret meetings. Then one day a handful of Bibles were smuggled in. I watched in awe as men and women held the books close to their chests and wept in gratitude. It was their first Bible, one with all its pages and written in their own language.

Maybe like me, you own several Bibles.

Maybe like me, you have a few Scriptures memorized.

Maybe, like me, you sometimes forget the power within the Bible.

161

Oh Jesus, I didn't see this one coming. I'm brokenhearted, and there are no words to express how we feel. You are our anchor and safe place. We need you today. Thank you for holding us close.

—Suzie

As I thought about the persecuted believers and their reaction, I realized it wasn't the cloth-bound books that caused so much emotion. It was that the words inside the books reflected the joy deep in their being. They had memorized the Word. The book they held in their hands was far more than a book. It was life-giving. It confirmed everything they already believed.

May I be honest with you? This chapter was going to be a lot more complex. When you are in a storm, you need all the tools available. You need shelter. Comfort. Strength. Direction. You need something to hold on to!

True to how we sometimes think, I was going to run in and grab the flashlight, the radio tuner, the blankets, the key to the shelter, the tarp . . . when what we really need is what feeds our soul so that when the storms hit, we are equipped.

When storms hit—and they will—everything we need is within the pages of God's Word.

I stood at a crossroads as I walked with Jesus in this part of my faith. I love the Bible. I know there's power in the Word. But is it *in* me?

Yes, to some degree. I've sat under great teaching. I've read my Bible. Journals are stacked in a neat row in my home containing words that leapt from its pages. I wondered what it would look like to have his words in my heart like a seed planted. To reach for the depth I saw in the persecuted believers' reaction to the Bible.

I longed to see his Word as the treasure that it is rather than a book lying in the backseat of my car or on the coffee table.

- Do we truly believe there is power in Scripture?
- Are we content to learn God's Word from others?
- Is it possible that there are tools—strength, truth, comfort, peace, assurance, direction, and so much more—that we are asking God for, and they are within the Bible's pages?
- Do we treasure his Word, or has it become familiar, perhaps even unessential?

My biggest fear in asking these questions is that this becomes just one more admonition to read your Bible. Instead, my prayer is that his Word comes alive inside of you.

When I was a teenager, I memorized Scripture, and those Scriptures still trip off my tongue as if I learned them yesterday. But it's been a long time since I've memorized anything. As I started memorizing the Word, I did so without pressure or a timeline. Sometimes it took a few days. Other times it came easily. I chose the first passage randomly, Jeremiah 17:7–8 (NLT):

> But blessed are those who trust in the Lord and have made the Lord their hope and confidence. They are like trees planted along a riverbank, with roots that reach deep into the water. Such trees are not bothered by the heat or worried by long months of drought. Their leaves stay green, and they never stop producing fruit.

A few weeks after I memorized this verse, Richard was diagnosed with cancer. This Scripture came to life throughout the next few months. We *were* in the heat. We were experiencing drought. Several times I found myself whispering these words:

Blessed are those who trust in the Lord.

> *Regardless of what is going on outside, the Word produces stability inside.*

I spoke at an event a couple of weeks before Richard's surgery. The audience didn't know I was dealing with insurance companies and paperwork and trying to figure out how we'd make it financially while he was recovering. They didn't know that the long-term side effects of his surgery weighed heavily on both of us as we made our decisions.

I was exhausted emotionally. If there had been a boat to carry me to the other side of the shore, I might have climbed in.

A woman approached me during dinner and handed me a small gift bag. "God spoke to me," she said. "I'm supposed to give you this." She walked away before I could say anything but a quick thank-you. The women's ministries director was calling my name to speak, so I tucked the gift under my chair. Later, I opened the bag.

Inside was a small, framed embroidered picture of a tree. Its roots were pushed deep into water. On the card she had written the Scripture from Jeremiah 17:7–8.

What a beautiful confirmation. She had no idea, but God knew what I needed.

Perhaps memorizing the Word isn't where you are. You long to understand the Bible better. This is your call to do just that. It might be with a group of women in your church or with a good friend over coffee. You might join an online study.

Start where you are, but don't stay where you are.

God's Word comes to mind just when you need it. It can show up in surprising ways—like when a stranger hands you a gift bag and you realize that God knows exactly where you are and what you need. As the thirteenth disciple, sit at his feet. Let him plant the Word in your soul.

Taking It Deeper

1. Describe how you felt God "in the boat" with you during an unexpected storm.

2. Read Romans 10:17. What does it mean to hear his Word? Is this the same for everybody? Why or why not?

3. In light of James 1:22, how can we be doers of the Word when a storm strikes?

4. *Calling out to Christ in the heart of a storm represents "good soil."* Do you believe that statement? Explain your answer.

5. Jesus came out of the wilderness filled to overflowing with the Spirit (Matthew 4:1–11).
   a. What does this teach you about the power of the Word?
   b. Is it for you too?

6. Colossians 3:16 encourages us to let the Word of God reside in us richly. Without making it a task, what is one way you could intentionally sit at Jesus' feet?

7. There are numerous ways to fill our hearts with the Word. One is an online Bible study (visit www.proverbs31.org/online-bible-studies for some good ones). What is another way to plant that seed inside of you?

Scripture

When your words came, I ate them; they were my joy and my heart's delight, for I bear your name, Lord God Almighty.

Jeremiah 15:16

Prayer

*Thank you for being in the boat with me, Jesus.
You and your Word are my anchor. Hold me
fast, Savior. Speak to the winds on my behalf.
Show me the power of your words.*

Living As a Disciple

- Give yourself permission to be honest that it's hard—and call that brave.
- Ask God to reignite your love for his Word.
- Begin to memorize Scripture, not as a duty, but so that your life reflects its words.
- Use whatever method works best for you (a journal, an app like Scripture Typer, Post-it Notes, etc.) to bury his teaching inside your heart.

10

Living What We Say We Believe

The hallmark of Christians in the first century was not their wealth. They had none. It was not their theology either. Their beliefs were so odd, religious people couldn't understand them. What gave them leverage was their inexplicable compassion and generosity. They had little, but they gave. They received little compassion, but they were willing to extend what they had to other people. They were hard to ignore.

Andy Stanley, *How to Be Rich*

She sat beside me on the plane. Her dress was new, with colors of red and orange and yellow so bright. She wore white sandals. Her wig was youthful, though her wrinkled face said that she was somewhere in her late seventies. She heaved a sigh of relief when the plane landed in Atlanta. With trembling hands she took out her tickets and thrust them in front of my face.

"What do I do next?"

I showed her the number of her next flight and promised I'd help find her gate on the monitor. She walked in front of me off the plane. Her gait was uneven, and I could tell her new shoes were pinching her feet something miserable. I pointed to the monitor and shared the gate number.

She repeated "B-22" at least ten times under her breath.

She took off down the crowded corridor of the Atlanta airport. The Atlanta airport is a hub, cram-packed with people on a slow day—but this was one of the busiest days, and people rushed and pushed their way to their next destination. I was a little concerned about my seatmate, but I knew she had the right gate number. I had told her how to find the escalator to the train. She left me and took a right into the bathroom.

Go in.

Follow a stranger into the bathroom? Was I supposed to stand outside her stall until she was through? She had made it clear she was good to go by going into the bathroom. She didn't say, "Wait here," or "I need your help." I continued to argue with myself silently. My window to catch my next flight was narrow because my previous flight had been delayed twice.

Which meant that her connection time might be just as narrow.

My gate was light-years from hers. We were bound for two different terminals. At this point I should have just stopped walking and gone in. I was arguing with myself, a clear sign that I knew what I was to do. Then I realized I had missed the exit for my train by ten gates.

Ten gates.

I spend a lot of time in airports. I've been in that airport a hundred times and know where the escalator to the train is located. I turned and ran back, knowing exactly the sight I would see.

And there she was.

That beautiful orange and red and yellow dress was moving toward me with that painful gait in a crowd of thousands. She arrived at the escalator at the same moment as I did. I let her climb on, and I fell in step just behind her.

"Hi," I said.

In her hand was a crumpled paper towel, soggy with her tears. Suddenly I saw the airport through her eyes. Five large terminals. Gates labeled with numbers and letters. Thousands of people, all busy and rushing. Signs with icons and arrows that pointed at crazy angles. Escalators hidden between fast food restaurants and bathrooms and more gates. A train with bells and a mechanical voice sounding out the next terminal number.

She hadn't gone into the bathroom just to use the facilities. She went in to have a good cry. "May I walk with you all the way to your gate?" I asked.

"I can't remember my gate number," she said, digging in her purse for her ticket.

"It's B-22," I said.

When we made it to her gate, she reached out her hand, and our fingers laced for just a second. I glanced at my phone to gauge the time, knowing that I had to leave. I said a quick good-bye and ran to my gate, praying I'd make it. As I ran, I thanked God for blinding me so that I walked ten gates out of my way . . . just for her. I thanked him for seeing a dignified older woman, crying in the bathroom, who needed help—and for not letting me go until I saw it too.

I thanked him for not allowing me to miss my assignment, even in my stubbornness.

▨ Let's Find Philip

Philip was a Galilean from the town of Bethsaida. He was one of the earliest believers in Jesus. He was first a disciple of John the Baptist, and it was likely he knew Andrew and Simon Peter, because they grew up in the same community.

Most of the first meetings between Jesus and the disciples seem almost happenstance. Jesus is walking along and sees a tax collector at his tax booth. One day he passes by John the Baptist, and two of JB's disciples follow him down the road.

Not so with Philip. Jesus went to find Philip.

Jesus was in Judea and had been baptized by John. He announced that he was going to Galilee, and while there he found Philip (John 1:43).

If he was looking for him, it meant that he'd met him before. If he's intentionally searching for him, there's a purpose. Let's slip into the moment when Jesus finds Philip.

He approaches him, and his first words are "Come with me."

Philip readily responds to Jesus' invitation. Then, in what we typically call a "new believer move," he runs to find his friend Nathanael. He can't wait to shout out the joyful news. "We've found him! He's the person Moses and the prophets wrote about. His name is Jesus, the son of Joseph from Nazareth."

Nathanael—later known as Bartholomew—soon becomes another of the twelve disciples.

▨ Come With Me

Why Tell Others?

I've heard people say that we should live our faith quietly. For some, they are afraid we'll do it all wrong. I understand that. There are times that we plow in with no regard for the person standing in front of us. We lead in with judgment when we've never taken a step in their shoes. Yet we are not without example on how to do this well.

Jesus was always sensitive to the Holy Spirit and to the human being standing in front of him. He purposefully walked into the lives of people and created relationship.

Somewhere there's a woman, a girl, a man, a people group—all who do not realize that Jesus loves them or sees them and that his love can change them forever.

Faith in God liberates from addiction. It heals hurts. It's a light in the dark places. It's strength. It's our comfort. It offers peace. It's wisdom. It's a one-on-one relationship with God that is beautiful and challenging.

Is it even possible to keep this to ourselves?

Then there are others who say that if you live a good life, people will notice and stumble toward Jesus because of that example. As a girl who didn't grow up in church, I don't think that happens for the majority of us. In fact, your goodness might just make me feel worse if I don't know Jesus or if my lifestyle doesn't seem to measure up to yours. Living a good life *is* reflective of Jesus, but it shows up when we care enough to talk about him and back that up with integrity and kindness and sacrificial love and in a thousand other noticeable ways.

Would I have found Jesus if people had quietly gone about their day and kept the good news from me? Would I have one day walked into a church to find out for myself?

I don't know the answer to that, but I am forever grateful that someone walked across the street to tell me about Christ.

There are millions of people who are not thinking about Jesus, but they are still just as valuable to the One who seeks them.

Then Jesus told them this parable: "Suppose one of you has a hundred sheep and loses one of them. Doesn't he leave the ninety-nine in the open country and go after the lost sheep until he finds it? And when he finds it, he joyfully puts it on his shoulders and goes home. Then he calls his friends and neighbors together and says, 'Rejoice with me; I have found my lost sheep.' I tell you that in the same way there will be more rejoicing in heaven over one sinner who repents than over ninety-nine righteous persons who do not need to repent."

Luke 15:3–7

Come With Me

When We Live Our Faith, We're Different

When we moved to a new state, we left friends and family and started over. I remember standing in church and looking around. We had been in the same community for our entire marriage. I looked at the people milling about, holding conversations.

"I don't know a soul," I told Richard. "Do you?"

We invited a couple to our home for dinner, and they quickly became friends. Jim is a lawyer and a pastor. I don't know how many times we've been talking and the conversation has fallen into the cracks of faith. Jim shares what God has spoken or done, or how his faith showed up in raw, hard places. These are not forced conversations. They spill out because it's such a part of who he is. He's a direct kind of guy, but his eyes well up as he shares the story and the God factor in it.

I see Jesus in Jim. So do others.

His wife is delightfully transparent. We'll be talking, and if Pam hears something that touches her deeply, she'll reach over and grab my hand. "God, show Suzie your power in this situation," she'll whisper. Then she'll let go of my hand, and we move on.

I see Jesus in Pam. So do others. She started a jig-tying company a few years ago, offering jobs to those who had no way of supporting themselves. She seeks out those who feel on the fringe. It's not unusual to see her pulling someone close and saying, "I love you"; she means it.

Living the gospel means that our relationship with Christ splashes out onto others.

Years ago someone *told* me about Christ. I was an angry, hurting teen and not receptive at all in the beginning. At some point, I followed her to church to see for myself. At the right time, faith rooted right in my heart. Things were still incredibly hard at home, but I saw Jesus in the people around me. They weren't perfect, nor did they pretend to be, but they were different.

This is why Jesus created such a stir as he walked the earth. If he had shown up and people followed and nothing changed . . . well, why bother with that guy? But that's not what happened. They followed, and passion for his teachings swelled among the ranks. Their new faith led them to pray with people, and that produced more passion.

It didn't stop there. It's easy to have passion, especially in the beginning when it's new and exciting. It was more deeply rooted than that. The early disciples continued to follow Jesus, even when it was hard.

The longer they walked with him, the more they began to sound like him and do like him, and that caused even more division.

This new faith went against custom. These guys healed on the Sabbath because the bruised human being calling out for help was greater than the rule. They gave respect to women, allowing them to sit and listen to Jesus' teaching rather than telling them it wasn't their place. These changes caused anger toward Jesus.

He was different.

The religious had lived good and moral lives for generations, and it had never caused a revolution of faith so real and relatable that it redefined what faith in God looked like and how we respond to it. That's what living the gospel can look like for you and me. When you begin to live the gospel—believing that what took place in the hearts of the disciples is for you too—it slips into your relationships. It shows up at work. It surprises you in a crowded airport when God shows you a woman on his heart. It's a very personal part of your faith that isn't featured in the Religion section of the newspaper, touting your good works for all the world to see. It's the everyday, raw act of listening to God and allowing him to show up as you cook dinner, as you water the lawn, as you work in an environment that might or might not be receptive to your faith, as you fill your gas tank, as you raise your children, as you work through conflict with your spouse or a friend.

Wherever you are.

Whatever you are doing.

No matter who is watching, or isn't.

Living the gospel invites faith to be an integral part of who you are.

Living the Gospel Creates a Domino Effect

If you asked me to list the top five people who influenced my faith, Jane would be one of them. When she passed away, I traveled to her funeral. Many of the people attending were from the church I attended as a girl, and I hadn't seen most of them in well over thirty-five years. I was asked to come early and eat with the family. I slipped in and said hello, gave lots of hugs, and was about to leave so they could gather and pray before the ceremony when I heard my name called out.

"Suzie! Hey, Suzie!"

It was Phillip, from youth group way back when.

"How's your mom?" he asked.

When Phillip knew me as a teen, my home was a mess. I briefly shared that my mom had been healed for a long time. I told him about her beautiful smile and how much I treasured my relationship with this strong, lovely woman. Then he asked about another person. It wasn't as easy to answer the next question. Things weren't fine. Prayers seemed to bounce back when I prayed for this person.

He asked me to sit, and he told me a story about a close friend of his.

This friend of Phillip's was a prayer warrior. Her life reflected years of talking to God, but her son was an addict. There wasn't anything that pointed to why he became an addict. His home life was good growing up. He knew about Jesus. He loved his family, but somewhere in his late teens he made poor choices that led to addiction, which led to prison numerous times.

God was a strong but gentle presence as she balanced loving her son but not protecting him in his addiction. One day she got a phone call from prison. Her son was ill. Years of addiction had caught up with him physically, and they were giving him no hope. It was time for his release, and he asked to come home.

She nursed her son for weeks until he passed away. On the day that he died, she received a phone call from someone who lived across country. He didn't know her son well, or that he had died, but he shared a remarkable vision he experienced in prayer that day.

In it, her son entered heaven. He dropped to his knees before Jesus. "I didn't do so good on earth," he said.

Jesus knelt and pulled him close. "You're going to be okay now, son."

As I listened to this story, I couldn't hold back the tears. What a beautiful image of grace. Phillip continued with his story. The man's mother later discovered that her son often ministered to others in prison. He freely admitted that he was a mess, but that he loved Jesus and always had. He hated the addictions that bullied him for far too many years, and he was ashamed that the only place he seemed to be able to live clean was behind prison bars. Many of the prisoners appreciated his gut-honest faith between a rock and a hard place—and they believed too.

We may never understand how far-reaching faith can be.

As I listened, I considered the domino effect of faith.

A mom's prayers did not go unnoticed.

A man's messy faith impacted men behind bars.

He died in her arms as she sang and prayed over him.

He entered heaven, tired from his earthly battle, but received by a loving Savior.

A friend made a phone call, and it encouraged a grieving mama.

Her story encouraged Phillip, who told me.

His retelling of that story took root in a deep cavern where I battled discouragement over a loved one. Phillip didn't even know he was on assignment that day, but the visual image of God's mercy over this son's life sparked dying flames inside of me. It reminded me of the possibilities of what can be, and perhaps even what might be taking place at that very moment because of prayer.

The majority of ministry shows up in the most natural of ways—seeing people as God sees them, hearing the voice of God, and responding in whatever way he leads.

> Thank you for seeing people differently than we do, and for opening my eyes. Today I believe that my prayers are not only heard, but working in this beautiful human being so broken and so loved by you.
>
> —Suzie

When we live out the gospel, it reaches to include others. I don't know if we'll ever fully understand how much until we stand before God in eternity and he shows us how the little assignments played out—not just in the life of one person, but far beyond our wildest imaginations.

Our Strengths Aren't Always Our Greatest Assets

Are you a test-taking girl like me? According to StrengthsQuest, my greatest strengths are intellection, input, positivity, empathy, and belief.

I'm a relational thinker with a strong core of beliefs.

When I take a spiritual gifts test, I find that my top five spiritual gifts are teaching, encouraging, discernment, wisdom, and giving. My lowest scores are in administration and service/helps.

Then there's the great book *The Five Love Languages* by Gary Chapman. When I took that test, I found that my love language is touch. I feel safe and loved when I am held close in the arms of those I love the most. So I'm a touchy-feely kind of girl.

Wow, that's a whole lot of information about me!

We take these kinds of tests to figure out what we're good at. It helps us understand why we like some things better than others, or why we clash with someone whose strengths are different from ours. These types of tests are useful—unless we allow them to become limitations. It would be easy for me to say, "I don't naturally excel at serving/helps. So you take this mop and bucket, because that's not my God-given job."

Pshaw!

Pushing that mop around might be right where God has placed me for that moment, whether it is to experience selfless service or because of the person who will be in the room with me.

> *God uses our strengths, but just as effectively, he uses our weaknesses.*

I'm a speaker, and I didn't walk willingly into that role. I've always admired those who step onto a stage and thrive speaking to crowds. As the years pass, there's less heart-hammering, but there's still nothing in me that says, "I got this. Watch me shine! Hear me roar!" Instead, I've learned to trust that God will take my preparation and prayers, and my heart to love others in his name, and show up with me when I speak. I still marvel when I step down and realize that the anointing on his word and over my heart far surpasses my naturally introverted personality.

I've come to love speaking because of that.

As his disciple, you will find that Jesus will take you beyond your strengths. I mentioned speaking, but he also called me to be a good mom when I wasn't sure how. He asked me to deal with conflict in a healthy way when I wanted to run from it. I could list several of my weak areas, but the bottom line is, we all have them. Jesus didn't run the disciples through a series of tests to find their strengths and then match them accordingly.

He knew their strengths, and he knows ours.

I believe that Jesus loved nothing more than watching one of the disciples discover what he was capable of. Just as much,

I believe he delighted in watching his strength show up in their weaknesses.

Get to know your strengths. Live them as much as you can, but don't underestimate how life-changing it is when God shows up in your weaknesses.

If he leads us into our weaknesses, it teaches us to depend on him. It grows us in areas that we wouldn't go on our own.

I now understand that I really do love being with people. I learned that from stepping into my weaknesses. Part of the battle was uncertainty, but there is also a very natural introverted thread running through my personality. Stepping into my weakness didn't change that, but I have become a learned extrovert.

Finding our strengths is helpful; living in his strength is empowering.

God moved me out from behind the keyboard of my laptop—my sweet spot—to stand in front of people. Engaging in conversation with strangers eventually felt comfortable and good, even adventurous. I discovered that most people are fascinating if given a chance to share their story. I still come home from speaking engagements and climb into a chair and wrap a blanket around me to fill back up after a weekend event. Then I speak again, because that's where following Jesus has unexpectedly led me.

When I tell people that I'm naturally shy, most are surprised, and I love that. That's where living the gospel has produced fruit that has nothing to do with me or my strengths but with his empowerment in my weak places.

Do you sense Jesus leading you to a place where it makes your knees weak? Don't underestimate the fact that he knows what you don't. That he sees inside of you what you might not. Trusting him in your weakness is living the gospel in its most intimate form. It takes you further than your faith can ever wander and where your trust is without borders.

Living the Gospel Helps You Find Your Part in the Miracle

Philip and the disciples have worked side by side with Jesus all day long. Late in the afternoon, Jesus says to Philip,

> "Where shall we buy bread for these people to eat?" He asked this only to test him, for he already had in mind what he was going to do. Philip answered him, "It would take more than half a year's wages to buy enough bread for each one to have a bite!"
>
> John 6:5–7

There are five thousand men in the crowd, which means that about twenty thousand are possibly in attendance once children and wives are included. Madison Square Garden is a multi-purpose indoor arena in the New York City borough of Manhattan. Crowds fill up the arena to watch professional hockey matches and listen to famous musical artists and bands. It's considered the world's most well-known arena. It holds 19,763 people at capacity. Jesus is preaching to a crowd that would fill every seat in Madison Square Garden, plus some.

When Philip presents the problem, Jesus says, "You give them something to eat" (Mark 6:37).

You feed them.

This was Philip's assignment. He was invited to find enough food to feed a crowd the size of a Madison Square Garden audience. It's an impossible assignment, at least on the surface.

Is Philip's assignment to feed every single person in that crowd? It isn't. It is to find a few loaves and fishes, and ask Jesus to multiply it however he wishes.

That's our call too.

That day in the airport, I was asked to slow down long enough to lead a woman to her gate. I don't know if she prayed in the bathroom for God to help her. I do know he cared. There were thousands in the airport that day. He didn't ask me to take care of every one of them.

I imagine that there were hundreds of assignments going on all around me. This was mine. To do only what he asked, which was originally to follow her into the bathroom, but overall to make sure she got to her gate safely.

We get to participate in miracles and answered prayers. The greatest opportunities are usually the closest. In our home. In our workplace. With that neighbor or friend. With a beleaguered pastor's wife. With that waitress who's working two jobs to feed her kids.

Sometimes our assignment is to give compassion and mercy to the person staring back at us in the mirror. We speak truth and life to ourselves. We show mercy. We stop when we've run into the end of ourselves and let his words become renewed life in our bones and spirit.

We're not alone as we live out the gospel. We are promised that the Holy Spirit will give us the words we need, or show us the heart of the Father in a given situation (John 14:16–17). He won't lead you astray.

Taking It Deeper

1. How is living the gospel different from serving in a ministry?

2. Where is it the most challenging to live the gospel? Why is that?

3. John 16:13 reminds us that the Holy Spirit guides us into
   _____.

4. John 16:14–15 promises that the Holy Spirit reveals _____
   to us and in us.

5. Read Galatians 5:22–23. What does the Holy Spirit produce inside of us? Describe one way that this might show
   up in your relationships with those closest to you.

6. Who told you about Jesus? Did that person tell you or show
   you, or both? Name one way this person most influenced
   you to become a believer.

7. In my own life, living out the gospel means [share your
   answer].

SCRIPTURE

For the Son of Man came to seek and save those who are
lost.

Luke 19:10 NLT

PRAYER
---

*Teacher and Lord, you showed by example how
to live the gospel. Let me begin to live my faith
in such a way that others see you inside of me,
especially in my home and with those closest*

to me. If there is anything lacking, light up the
Holy Spirit inside of me to show me the way.

LIVING AS A DISCIPLE

- Redefine ministry to include the everyday.
- Follow where Jesus leads *you*.
- Ask the Holy Spirit to help you in your weaknesses.

11

Walking Into the Deep

He had made the planets and shaped the stars, yet he
prayed. He is the Lord of angels and Commander of
heavenly hosts, yet he prayed. He is coequal with God,
the exact representation of the Holy One, and yet he
devoted himself to prayer. He prayed in the desert,
cemetery, and garden.

Max Lucado, *Before Amen: The Power of a Simple Prayer*

I understand the significance of prayer. Yet my definition of
prayer changed as I walked with the disciples and observed
Jesus. There were untapped depths to this thing we call prayer.
This is where my theology was turned upside down.

Several years ago I traveled to El Salvador with a team, and
we went to the beach. It wasn't a public beach. There were no
warning signs or markers. Just untainted stretches of black

lava sand and broken shells, and a couple of volcanos in the background. I was edging closer to the rippling waves when I heard a shout behind me and turned to see one of the locals waving his arms wildly. I felt a whoosh. A massive wave pulled me under, and I spiraled under the water, scooping up sand in my shorts and bathing suit, in my ears and nose. When the water finally subsided, I lay flat on the beach. I had picked up what felt like twenty pounds of sand in my clothing and in my nose, ears, and eyes. I couldn't see. I couldn't hear. But I could breathe through my mouth.

Thank you, God. I can breathe.

I gulped air through my mouth and whispered those words in my blind and deaf state. Arms pulled me to a standing position as friends pounded on my back and turned my head to remove sand from my ears. For several days after that I sneezed black lava sand, and when I washed my hair, I felt sand filtering out of my ears. I wasn't the only one hit by the dangerous wave from nowhere. The force of the wave surprised several of my friends and skipped them across jagged rocks and crushed seashells like stones across the surface of a pond, earning many of them nasty scrapes and gashes.

Locals saw what we did not. There was a dangerous tide stirring just under the rippling waters, waiting to crash onto shore. Until that day I'd always loved the ocean, and I still do, but I gained respect for the depths of power that my eyes could not see.

That most accurately describes what changed for me on this journey.

Prayer became more than talking to God throughout my day or twirling in my living room in gratitude. These are beautiful aspects of prayer, and I treasure them, but there's an untapped force to prayer that most of us fail to grasp.

In no way do I see prayer as dangerous for those who practice it. Instead, I see it as dangerous for the enemy of our soul.

Do you desire more than a formula teaching you how to pray? Amazing teachers and preachers and scholars have taught us ways that we can talk with God.

> *We can communicate with God, but we are invited to commune with him.*

I want more than a formula. I want to hear him back.

I long to see its effects in my belief system and over my life.

Jesus often led the disciples from *how* to the *why*.

Why did Jesus pray? As the Son of God, and part of God himself, he could communicate without words, but he pulled himself away from the disciples to commune with God. He sought the presence of his Father. He was restored and filled up and empowered.

Is that for us too?

The difference between communicating our needs or wants or prayer requests and communing with God is that one is talking to him, while the other becomes a conversation—but more so a connection.

Learning More About James, Son of Alphaeus

James is referred to as James the Less or Lesser, but only to distinguish him from the other disciple named James. I don't know how fun it would be to be called "less" to distinguish me from another person on the team. The Greek word is *mikros*, which means smaller in stature, so James was most likely shorter in height than the other disciple named James. He's mentioned in the gospels, but only in the lists of disciples. There are no recorded feats or conversations other than a mention in 1 Corinthians 15 in one of Paul's letters to the church of Corinth.

> The first thing I did was place before you what was placed so emphatically before me: that the Messiah died for our sins, exactly as Scripture tells it; that he was buried; that he was raised from death on the third day, again exactly as Scripture says; that he presented himself alive to Peter, then to his closest followers, and later to more than five hundred of his followers all at the same time, most of them still around (although a few have since died); that he then spent time with James and the rest of those he commissioned to represent him; and that he finally presented himself alive to *me*.
>
> 1 Corinthians 15:3–8 THE MESSAGE

The church of Corinth was established on Paul's second missionary journey, but things were not going well. Like in a bad reality TV show, believers battled one another over minute details, even to the point of going to court. They argued, they debated, and it seemed that the church might fall apart. Paul wrote the letter to the church of Corinth to remind them of the good news he had preached to them in the beginning.

Paul was born ten years after Jesus' death, so he never met Jesus physically. He did, however, hear Jesus' voice on the road to Damascus. That one encounter completely altered Paul's entire life. He had been trying to destroy the church, but then he became a driving force behind building the church. He lived the gospel whether he was sitting across the table from friends or bound in chains in jail. He went on to tell the church of Corinth:

I don't deserve to be included in that inner circle, as you well know, having spent all those early years trying my best to stamp God's church right out of existence.

1 Corinthians 15:9 THE MESSAGE

Paul wanted the church to know that one conversation with Jesus changed him forever. He was a praying man before he heard the voice of Jesus, because he was a religious man. But he swam into deeper waters in his faith because of Jesus, and those prayers changed from religious rote to relationship. He prayed for people, and they were healed in the name of Jesus! He discovered this truth in Jesus' words to the Twelve:

Very truly I tell you, whoever believes in me will do the works I have been doing, and they will do even greater things than these, because I am going to the Father.

John 14:12

What about James? Why is he mentioned by Paul in his letter to the Corinthians? Is it significant?

My first question after examining this passage was, "Is this James the son of Alphaeus?" The other disciple named James had already died as the first martyr, so that ruled him out. Some have said that this is James the brother of Jesus, but he wasn't one of the commissioned. So most land on the fact that Paul is referring to James the son of Alphaeus.

James didn't just come face-to-face with Jesus after the resurrection. Jesus spent time with him.

Spending time with Jesus assured James that following him had not been a mistake. Everything that he was told by Jesus was true. These gifts were found in the presence of Jesus, one-on-one.

That's our inheritance as well. We can pray religiously, or we can commune with our Savior and feel his Spirit alive within our religious dead bones.

Come With Me

Untapped Power

I ran smack into the end of myself recently. I was juggling words and deadlines and pressing family needs and a house that needed cleaning, and "boom"—I was all out of me.

There were too many people that I loved and too little time. It was just a season, but one with too many emails. Too many projects. Too many tasks. I hate running into the end of me, yet it's where I often begin to reach for more of God.

Jesus prayed often. There were times he pulled an all-nighter. Other times he prayed in great earnest. He already has an all-access pass to the heart of God, yet he sought God.

> And a woman was there who had been subject to bleeding for twelve years, but no one could heal her. She came up behind him and touched the edge of his cloak, and immediately her bleeding stopped.
>
> "Who touched me?" Jesus asked.
>
> When they all denied it, Peter said, "Master, the people are crowding and pressing against you."
>
> But Jesus said, "Someone touched me; I know that power has gone out from me."
>
> Luke 8:43–46

Jesus emanated power. He was so full to the brim that a bleeding and desperate woman's touch in faith healed her. He stopped to see what had taken place. His disciples thought him mad, because he was pressed in on every side by a large crowd. He emanated power, but his heavenly Father was the Source. It's a pattern we find with Jesus. He pours out and pours out, but he also pours in and pours in.

There were many times he'd take the fatigued disciples to a grove of olive trees and leave them at a distance while he communed with God.

Sometimes I let power leak from me, dripping it, pouring it, splashing it as if there is a never-ending supply. There are no desperate women crawling through a crowd to touch the hem of my garment. But our elderly and much-loved parents are facing struggles, and we don't always know the best thing to do, but they need us. I have adult children who are amazing parents, but they need a break from time to time. Sometimes they need advice. Then there is a rambunctious, beautiful cluster of grandbabies all under the age of five who want all of me when I am with them.

We all leak constantly.

When I was a younger parent, I often came home from work and kicked off my high heels as I transitioned from one job to another. I made dinner, washed dishes, herded kids to the table to finish homework, and made them take baths. I sat on bleachers and watched endless games on Saturdays, cheering in the rain, baking in the sun. I drove from school events to church events to sporting events, praying for the day they'd drive themselves, even as I longed to treasure their younger years.

Beyond my family, I have leaked emotionally and spiritually like a stretched-out balloon as I worked or served in ministry. I know how to say no, and I do, but I was exactly where I needed to be. The problem was that I sometimes failed to stop and fill back up.

For most of us, a lot of yeses are nonnegotiable. So we keep on doing. We keep on going. We keep on pouring out until there's nothing left. That's our life and we wouldn't trade it for anything, but then we run smack into empty and we wonder why.

Jesus was God. He could have simply continued on, but he didn't.

That's the untapped power in prayer. When we seek him, we find the Source. He's present in our every day. He's alive in our fatigue. He's thriving in us despite our lack of wisdom as he shows us the next step, the next word, what to do or what not to do, how to prioritize or when to simply stop. He is active in our ministry or parenting or loving others. He assures us that, though we might not be heard by others, he is listening.

Jesus sought God as much as he poured out to others.

If something is untapped, it means that it is available. That's exciting news. It's also a choice point. Do we tap in to it, or is our natural tendency to . . .

- spend a lot of time and energy in things that offer little in exchange
- just keep filling up our empty places with more activity
- keep on going until fatigue shows up in unexpected and unwanted ways
- consider prayer as something we mark off our list for the day, and move on

Jesus never lost sight of his identity because of the untapped power in prayer. He sought God because he was the Son of God.

We are daughters of the Most High God. This is not a task. There's no set formula. It's not a "you should." It's what we desperately need.

191

What Does It Mean to Pray?

One day the disciples asked Jesus to teach them to pray (Luke 11:1). These were good Jewish boys. They watched their fathers and grandfathers pray three times daily, four times on the Sabbath, and additional times on other special days. They followed the same religious practices when they became men at the tender age of thirteen.

They knew *how* to pray.

They didn't need a lesson on the practice of prayer, but they were asking Jesus to connect them with God in the way Jesus connected with him. Jesus offered the disciples a framework of prayer in his answer (Luke 11:2–4). It's simple and beautiful.

Lord, I praise you.

Meet my basic needs.

Forgive me for my sins and help me to forgive others.

Deliver me from evil.

Lord, I praise you.

They had asked him to teach them to pray as John the Baptist had taught his followers, and he did. But he took it deeper (Luke 11:9–13).

Keep on knocking.

Keep on seeking until the door is opened.

If your earthly daddy gives you good gifts, how much more will your heavenly Father give the Holy Spirit to those who ask him?

And there it is. The one thing he wanted to give that we may never seek. It was the offer to brim and splash with the power of his Spirit.

God in us.

Jesus *alive* in us.

The Spirit working through us.

Of all the things we ask for in prayer, do we ask for his power? On the other side of empty is full. I thought life would slow down when my kids left. It didn't. I thought life would slow down when I hit a certain age. It hasn't. I don't know that it ever will, and I'm not sure that I'm looking to live a sedentary life following Jesus, because there is uncharted territory ahead of me.

We need his power and are asked to pull away and walk into his presence to find what we need.

Untapped Revolution

The deep is where Jesus declared war against the enemy. He carried his doubts about suffering, the real emotions provoked by the scallywags that followed him wherever he went. It's where his fatigue and battle scars were safely revealed to the eyes of his Father.

He walked out filled (Mark 1:35; Luke 4:14; 6:12).

I've walked into the deep before, many times. Usually it is reserved for when I am in battle. It's my go-to when nothing is going right and I wave my white flag because I'm out of answers. I've done all that I can.

Following Jesus' example changed that. He sought God often. I began to look for him in the good-things-that-happen-to-good-people part of my life rather than in the waiting. I recognized my need to fill up spiritually when my reserve was at three-quarters of a tank instead of when the light flashed empty, empty, empty.

At first I wasn't sure what this should look like. Like Paul, and maybe like you, I knew *how* to pray. I understood the importance of prayer. I had also somehow associated prayer with getting something in return. Not things or material goods, but to always feel his presence (and if I didn't, I assumed something was wrong with me or God wasn't listening).

Perhaps that's why hanging out with God—talking with him while driving, sending up a sincere prayer of gratitude, whispering to him while rocking a child to sleep—are comfortable and familiar territory for me. It's a good place, and one that I treasure. One that I'll continue to seek in my relationship with him.

There were no grenades thrown or hand-to-hand combat with the enemy, but I was walking into very different territory as I watched Jesus' example.

Prayer offers untapped revolution.

At the Last Supper Jesus warns Peter, "The enemy wants to sift you like wheat" (see Luke 22:31).

Jesus has pleaded in prayer for Peter. He knows the battle ahead. Later that night Jesus goes to the Mount of Olives. He leaves the men and moves just a stone's throw away to pray. There Jesus agonizes in prayer, and an angel comes to strengthen Jesus. When he is through communing with his heavenly Father, he finds the disciples asleep. They are exhausted by grief (Luke 22:45). When they awake, they stumble into the garden only to watch Judas plant the traitorous kiss on Jesus' cheek.

Suffering begins for Jesus. Persecution begins for the disciples. They are launched into spiritual warfare on a level they will not completely understand until later.

Come on, guys, pray.

These are words of compassion. He understands that there is an enemy who desires to sift them like wheat. If we focus on the

I don't know when it happened, but prayer became methodical rather than personal. Today I felt you, Jesus. Your power. Your incredible powerful and sweet presence.

—Suzie

enemy factor alone in this story, it might lead us to unhealthy or unbalanced faith.

There *is* an enemy, yes. Jesus' response to that enemy was prayer. Prayer counters the one who dares to damage the heart and faith of one of God's own.

The disciples took a nap.

Have I been taking a nap spiritually? There is no guilt in this question, just an awakening of what is available.

Come on, Suzie, pray.

Come on, [put your name here], pray.

The enemy desires to sift each of us like wheat, but there's untapped revolution that rises up against him when we commune with God.

> *Prayer changes things, but it ultimately changes the one who prays.*

Untapped Transformation

One morning I was on my way upstairs to my home office. *Come with me.*

Did you know that he speaks to us? It's that quiet, persistent nudge inside that won't go away. I slowed on the stairs and then settled into a quiet place. Normally the pressure of what I need to do lingers around the edges, but it fell away. I felt God in my home. The leaks were being filled. His tangible, sweet presence washed into that room. I didn't want to leave. My deadlines no longer beckoned louder than my longing for him.

It's not always like that. I wish it were, but that's the point of walking into the deep. It's not going in with expectations, but expectancy.

Whatever you have for me, God.

Whatever I have, I offer you.

Oswald Chambers, in *My Utmost for His Highest*, says about prayer:

> Prayer is not a normal part of the life of the natural man. We hear it said that a person's life will suffer if he doesn't pray, but I question that. What will suffer is the life of the Son of God in him, which is nourished not by food, but by prayer. When a person is born again from above, the life of the Son of God is born in him, and he can either starve or nourish that life.[1]

We can acknowledge that prayer isn't a normal part of the life of a natural woman. Perhaps you've been walking into the deep for a long time, but even you know that there are times when we sit and wait for his presence and we feel nothing. It doesn't mean that he's not there. It doesn't mean that he's not listening. What a beautiful gift to simply show up because you want to be with him. But there's more. Chambers goes on to say:

> Prayer is the way that the life of God in us is nourished. Our common ideas regarding prayer are not found in the New Testament. We look upon prayer simply as a means of getting things for ourselves, but the biblical purpose of prayer is that we may get to know God Himself.[2]

What are our common ideas about prayer? I asked several women.

- "I pray for my loved ones."
- "I pray because I need his provision."
- "I pray because I'm supposed to as a believer."
- "I pray because I'm desperate."

These were only a few of the hundreds of responses. Not one of them said, "I pray because it changes me."

That's what contrasts with Jesus' example in the New Testament. He didn't want to suffer beatings and nails in his hands and feet (who would?), but his prayer was, "Change my heart to reflect yours in this matter."

Powerful! There's untapped transformation as we walk into the deep.

The temptation will be to make this a chore or to set up a chart. If that's what works for your personality, go for it, but understand that the strongest of relationships are often deepened by merely showing up.

I'm here because I love you.

I'm here because I know there's even more depth in this relationship, and I want all of it.

I'm here and it's a good day, and I want absolutely nothing more than to be with you.

I'm crazy busy and pulled in fifty different directions, but you are my priority.

Show up. He promises to be there when you do (1 John 5:14).

TAKING IT DEEPER

1. Read Ephesians 3:12. What words describe how you approach God in prayer? Don't think of them as negative or positive words, but as honest words.

2. Sometimes we put so much pressure on prayer (what it should be, what we say) that we stay away from prayer. Share your experience.

3. Why do you think Jesus pulled away from the disciples to talk with God on a personal level? What does his example show you?

4. Read Matthew 12:27–29. The crowd recognized power in Jesus. How does he explain the source of this power?

5. What is the difference between seeking God when you have a need and seeking him when life is good?

6. Suzie says, "The other side of empty is full." Describe your reaction to that statement.

SCRIPTURE

But Jesus often withdrew to lonely places and prayed.

Luke 5:16

PRAYER

I've been asleep, Jesus, and there are deep places yet to travel in my relationship with you. Wake me up to the power of prayer.

LIVING AS A DISCIPLE

- Pour in as much as you pour out.
- Take the pressure off of prayer.
- Pursue it simply because he meets you there.

12

Go . . . and Give

Several years ago Richard went on a mission trip to South Africa. He came home in love with the country. Evidently the people he met liked him too, and a ministry job offer followed. I didn't doubt that South Africa and its people were lovely, but it was exactly 9,275 miles away as the crow flies (according to Siri). Our children were in college. I loved our empty nest, but I expected they'd fly back from time to time. I'd love to pretend that I instantly said yes and never looked back, but this mama's heart fought with the thought of not seeing my children but once a year.

Richard and I each prayed about this opportunity, and when I did, there was nothing, zilch, nada. Was I missing his leading?

I longed to be open to wherever God might be leading, but utter silence wasn't the response I expected.

One night I dreamed that we made the move, and I woke up with my pillow soaked with tears. I slipped into my husband's arms. "I don't think we're supposed to go."

It was more than my mama's heart; it wasn't for us. Time passed and the feeling ebbed. The combination of a current job he didn't like and the adventure of living in South Africa made the offer enticing, but if God wasn't in it, then it wasn't for us.

We know that Jesus told us to go, but how do we know where or how, or what that looks like?

> And Jesus came up and spoke to them, saying, "All authority has been given to Me in heaven and on earth. Go therefore and make disciples of all the nations, baptizing them in the name of the Father and the Son and the Holy Spirit, teaching them to observe all that I commanded you; and lo, I am with you always, even to the end of the age."
>
> Matthew 28:18–20 NASB

This call to go can be confusing. We want to go, but does that mean we pack up and move to Africa or Indonesia? For many, that's exactly where it leads, but that same calling leads just as many international missionaries to the United States, because we are in need of Jesus too.

Abraham Kuyper, a Dutch theologian, said, "There is not a square inch in the whole domain of our human existence over which Christ, who is Sovereign over all, does not cry: 'Mine!'"[1]

Going is not a place; it's joining with Jesus to make this a reality.

This unfolds as we go . . . and as we discover how to give.

Let's Get to Know Bartholomew, AKA Nathanael

Let's get to know our last disciple. Do you remember when Philip raced to find his friend Nathanael? Let's go back to that moment.

Philip races to find his friend. He's just met Jesus. Philip is certain that Jesus is the Messiah, but Nathanael is not so sure.

"How could anything good come from Nazareth?" he says (see John 1:46).

There are cities that have poor reputations, whether they deserve them or not. You hear the name of the city, and all kinds of negative images are associated. Nazareth had a poor reputation. It was a small and insignificant agricultural village, with no trade routes. With all of Galilee to choose from, why would the Messiah come from Nazareth?

"Come and see for yourself," Philip says.

The two friends walk until they find where Jesus is staying. As they approach, Jesus calls out to Nathanael. "Here he is. A genuine son of Israel, a man of integrity."

"How do you know me?" Nathanael asks.

"I saw you under the fig tree before Philip found you."

"You are the son of God!" Nathanael says excitedly.

"Do you believe just because I told you I had seen you under a fig tree?" Jesus replies. "You will see greater things than this."

What an odd conversation, but what an illustration of the relationship between mankind and God. Jesus knew Nathanael long before Nathanael was aware that Jesus existed. When he told Nathanael that he was a genuine son of Israel, he wasn't referring to his ancestry, but to his character. Jesus *knew* him. He was mindful of him. Our God is mindful of every individual on earth. That's staggering. I've stood in crowds before and wondered how it was possible that he loved each and every one.

Nathanael becomes a follower of Jesus that day. Eventually he is named as one of the twelve disciples, and his given name of Nathanael becomes Bartholomew, which means "gift of God."

That relationship caused Nathanael to "go." He traveled to India with a copy of the gospel of Matthew.

He also gave. Nathanael, like ten of his fellow original disciples, was martyred for his faith.

Giving Means That We Stop Hoarding

I stood in the garage, which was stacked with ramshackle boxes filled with discarded clothes and cracked garden hoses. Old cans of pesticide stood next to empty gas cans. Tools and fishing rods were stacked against the wall. I went inside the home. The wallpaper was faded, except for blocks of color where family photos once hung. There were tables of knick-knacks and glass figurines alongside pots and pans and paperback books in different rooms of the house.

I don't get to go to them very often, but I love estate and yard sales.

Cars were lined up and down the street, and the yard and home were crowded with people looking over the goods of this sale. I was on my way out when I saw a table of hats labeled Stetson. The hats were gorgeous and in mint condition. I don't buy a lot when I go junking. I might come home with an old book, but I'm more of a looker. But those hats captured my attention.

When they finally auctioned the hats, there were only a couple of bids, and I won the right to choose the pick of the lot. I was shocked when I went to pick up my hat and the clerk handed a large box across the counter.

"I'm supposed to choose one," I told him.

I don't care about hoarding things, God, but I definitely want to hoard people. I want to hold them tight and make sure they are never in harm's way. I want them close to me, where I can touch them and hear their voice and wrap my arms around them. Holding my people loosely is a sacrifice, but you have a plan for them because you love them even more than I do. Remind me not to hoard, but to be their greatest encourager as they follow you.

—Suzie

He pushed another large box my way. "You were bidding on the entire lot," he said. "Congrats. You've just bought yourself a whole heap of hats."

I laughed as I packed the boxes in my small car. What in the world was I going to do with all these hats? I kept one and sold the rest on eBay and made a killing.

Estate sales are fun, but they are also eye-opening to how we tend to hoard, even if we aren't on a reality TV show. There's a lot of stuff that we pay dearly for, care for, store, stack, and treasure. Thousands pay an extra fee to store what doesn't fit in the garage or in a home's storage space. Then one day when we're gone and all that stuff is tossed in boxes, people riffle through it to buy it for pennies on the dollar.

We'll be looking down from heaven when we finally get it.

That stuff was never the real treasure after all.

For years I struggled with holding tightly to what I had. I gave in the church offering because I was supposed to—but it was out of obedience rather than with pleasure. There's a difference. It doesn't take a lot to understand the root of my giving issues. I was on my own at seventeen years old. I was responsible for me, and every penny counted. I worked two jobs in high school, and also at the community college, where I earned a tuition waiver but needed to pay for room and board and books.

Well after I became a believer and into my adult years, I mentally existed as if my next dollar might be my last. Over time, I realized this was less about being stingy or selfish and more about stability. I held on tight because when I was younger and on my own, if I didn't, I'd lose my ride to work or not have a safe place to live or not have necessities like soap or food. It was an area that needed healing.

Can I share something? I didn't know how freeing it would be to give freely rather than to give grudgingly. It changed my attitude toward things. They weren't my security. The less I held tightly, the less hold that emotion had on my being.

We hoard (hold tightly to) for a reason. It might be greed. It might be selfishness. It might be that we really love something, or we want to give it to our children later on. We might hold on out of fear. We might hold on because of sentiment. There are many reasons to hold tight to things or money.

Yet the more we hold them loosely, the less those things define us. They're gifts. They still bring pleasure or security, but they mean less to us than what happens when we place all that we have in his hands.

As God healed my heart, I learned to hold financial security loosely. I pay my bills. I believe in a savings account. I want to be smart about retirement. But what's in my bank account isn't mine entirely. If I sense God asking me to give above a tithe for missions or to help translate Bibles for the remaining two thousand people groups who do not have access to a Bible in their language, it's his. And there's pleasure in watching him take a thousand different givers and use their gifts for his purposes.

In chapter three we met Ashley and Andrew. They believe that their home, their car, and every dollar they earn belongs to God. That can feel like a radical concept. Another couple I know drives a car with 300,000 miles on it because they are sending a young woman to college—a woman whose mom never could have sent her. They don't resent that their friends have a really nice vehicle; they see this as an eternal investment.

God will show you what he wants, for he speaks with us one-on-one. It begins as we shift into living as if everything we own belongs to him anyway.

Let's take this deeper.

I sat in a church and watched a baby dedication. Parents held wriggling babies in their arms and prayed this prayer: *God, lead our son (or daughter) to the corners of the earth if it is your desire. Let us show this child your love, and release him to your will for his life.*

That's a beautiful prayer, but it surprised me. If you put it into practice, it's more than a prayer. It's saying that this child you love, who gives you sweet kisses and races through the house without his clothes, squealing as you shout out, "Naked baby on the loose!" is on temporary loan.

That's the heart of giving. Our finances might send someone where we cannot go. It might help build a children's wing of a church. It might feed or educate a child. That's between us and God. He'll show us our part. After the baby dedication, my prayers changed over my children, and especially my grandchildren.

I give them to you. Wherever you lead them. Whatever you desire for their lives.

Praying that over my life is an adventure. Praying it over my family is a sacrifice. It's holding up open hands where I want to hold tight.

Giving means to release. To give without strings. To live as if everything we have is his. When we do that, we will one day come to the end and realize that the treasure we've accumulated isn't going to be sitting on a table at an estate sale.

It's affecting eternity.

We Give Our Plans

When it was time for college, she didn't want to leave home. College was only a half hour away, and she could drive it easily. Her family was a lot of fun and home was comfortable, so why leave?

Her parents pushed gently, and with a tumble she fell out of the nest. She moved into the dorm, and when a campus ministry talked about an upcoming trip to Ukraine, she raised the funds and off she went. She was hooked. The next year she lived overseas for several months to serve a missionary family as a nanny. When that ended, she returned home, finished her degree, and settled into her plan for her life. She started teaching; she married; he became a pastor; they had children.

It was exactly how she planned.

One summer she and her husband went on a mission trip together. They started dreaming about serving as missionaries, with an understanding that it would be far in the future. They had children to raise and debts to pay. They were in their thirties, and there was a lot of time ahead. But soon they were approached about an open position in missions. She started to think about what it might be like to live in the country she had visited earlier, or somewhere similar. It was almost exciting!

When the missions director met with them, however, it wasn't what she expected. He told them stories of a country currently at a zero-conversion level. Less than 1 percent of the region's population was Christian, and those who practiced did so at a danger to themselves and their families.

Her heart sank. This was not the plan. It was one of the last places she'd want to go willingly. They were not expected to give an answer quickly. Over the next several weeks she started reading about the people. She started to see their faces. She started reading about the culture. As if he had taken her by the hand, she sensed that God was introducing her to his love for the country and its people. For a girl who once struggled to move twenty-five miles from home, this seemed like a big ask.

Going isn't where we go, but what happens as we do.

I'll go.

I'll give you my plans. I give you me.

That was her response. Today she and her husband and children serve in a country she had never thought about before God revealed it to her. When they were raising financial support for their new role as missionaries, they fielded a lot of questions. The questions were sincere, and this couple had already asked them all as they made their decision.

The only answer they gave was that they felt called to go, and they were glad they had said yes. It wasn't going to be easy, but it's exactly what they were supposed to be doing.

Jesus launched the disciples into the unknown, and he messed with their plans.

Tell them about me.

Tell them what you witnessed.

Tell them what you heard.

Make disciples.

When we give him our plans, we give him ourselves. In the beginning of this chapter I shared that my calling wasn't to go to South Africa, but my faith has led me to places and to people and in ministry in ways that I may have never chosen for myself. For my friend, her calling redefined the word *home* to include a zero-conversion region.

Giving him our plans is giving him ourselves.

Plan and prepare, because that's a smart way to live. But remember that our plans never trump his. Watching my friend's journey was fascinating.

I love that God chose a girl who once struggled to leave home to attend college thirty minutes away to travel across the world. As she did so, these words were added to her resume: *brave, tenacious, trusting, dependent on God, adventurous.*

Going begins with giving.

We give all that we own, all that we have, and all that we are.

Taking It Deeper

1. Do you agree that going is giving? Why or why not?

2. Suzie described living with open hands. How is this possible?

3. How can we be wise as we do so?

4. Suzie described holding tight to all that she had. What might this look like?

5. The word *give* means to let go, to give freely without strings. Describe one thing you sense God asking you to give.

6. Read John 17:6–19. This is Jesus' final prayer over the Twelve. Name three things he prayed over them.

7. Read John 17:20–26. In this same prayer, Jesus prayed over all of those who would hear the disciples' message. Name at least one thing Jesus desired for those who didn't yet know him or the Father.

SCRIPTURE

And this gospel of the kingdom will be preached in the whole world as a testimony to all nations, and then the end will come.

Matthew 24:14

PRAYER

Jesus, it's not about where I go, but about loosely holding all that I am and everything that I have. It's a daring prayer, I know, but I pray it with a full heart.

LIVING AS A DISCIPLE

- Be aware of what you hold tightly, and why.
- If giving is a struggle, ask God for his help.
- Leave room in your plans for heavenly redirection.

13

We Are the Thirteenth Disciple

I was visiting North Carolina, and my friend Lynn Cowell invited a couple of friends to come over. We sat in Lynn's living room with our Bibles open. Our friend Leah read a devotion about anointing she had written that past week. That's when something special happened. I can't explain it, except to say that the One we were talking about seemed to be in the room with us.

"I'm going to get my anointing oil," Lynn said.

My first thought was, *Who has anointing oil on hand, just like that?*

My second thought was *Yes!*

Lynn anointed each of us with oil, and we prayed for each other. There are markers in your faith where you're just rolling along, and suddenly you come face-to-face with the beauty of God. This was one of those times. The presence of God was in that room, so real that I felt as if I could reach out and touch him. A few moments after we ended our prayers, Renee, another friend in ministry, knocked on the door.

Over lunch we shared with her what had happened.

"I need it," she said.

Right?

We *need* it. We want to know Jesus, to hear the heartbeat of our heavenly Father. We desire to feel the Holy Spirit leading us, teaching us, showing us how to live the gospel in ways that draw others to him, delightfully transforming us forever. We want to be able to talk to him in the midst of doing laundry or when it's been an incredibly hard day. We want to hear his voice and respond to his leading. That's why I began this walk in the book of Luke. I had no idea at the time that it was anything other than a faith journey.

As I walked with the original disciples, I slowly began to tiptoe into faith that challenged and changed me. To hear the words of Jesus as I read the book of Luke and then purposely walked into the books of John, Matthew, and Mark.

I remember laughing as I read John 20. It was the scene shortly after Mary found the tomb empty and told John and Peter.

> Peter and the other disciple started out for the tomb. They were both running, but the other disciple outran Peter and reached the tomb first.
>
> John 20:3–4 NLT

Somewhere over the past year, John had become more than a flat character in a Bible story. He was three-dimensional. Real. That same guy whose mom wanted him and his brother to sit on either side of Jesus now made sure that the whole world knew two things as he recorded these events.

1. I'm the disciple that Jesus loved (John 20:2).

2. I beat Peter in the footrace.

Still competitive. Still wanting to be first. Yet mightily used of God. Hopeful. He was instrumental, along with Peter and a few others, in changing the world in Jesus' name. This footrace delighted me more than if John had arched his chin in the air with religious authority and said, "Of course. I knew it would happen all along."

They were so human.

Over that year, I not only watched as these men gained flesh-and-blood status, but I started to truly identify myself as the thirteenth disciple. Not in a weird, out-there way. Rather, I began to view my ordinary life and the decisions I made in light of my faith in God.

I no longer looked at life the same way. If I had to name the greatest lesson I learned over this past year, it would be this:

Walking with Jesus moves us out of the external to the eternal.

It's amazing how much of ourselves we invest in things that aren't going to matter when we look back at our lives. Some of the things that took up a lot of shelf space in my heart moved to make room. If it's tied to eternity, then I saw it differently—whether material things or the definition of success or people.

I have never felt like I fit more perfectly in my faith. Yet I realize how much more there is to learn and experience as his disciple. You and I are the thirteenth disciple.

The rest of this chapter is the beginning of your story.

Step into the crowd and listen to his words.
Come with me.
Wherever I lead you.
Whatever the price.
Do you say yes?

Notes

Introduction

1. "God Gave Us the Bible to Transform Us," Daily Hope With Rick Warren, May 21, 2014, http://rickwarren.org/devotional/english/god-gave-us-the-bible-to-transform-us.

Chapter 1: But If You Say So

1. G. Campbell Morgan, *The Gospel According to Luke* (Old Tappan, NJ: Fleming H. Revell, 1931), 73.

Chapter 2: You Don't Mean Me, Do You?

1. Patsy Clairmont, *I Grew Up Little: Finding Hope in a Big God* (Nashville: Thomas Nelson, 2004), 3.

2. Beth Moore, *To Live Is Christ* (Nashville: B&H Publishing, 2001), Kindle edition, loc. 1902.

3. Quoted in Leslie T. Lyall, *A Passion for the Impossible: The Continuing Story of the Mission Hudson Taylor Began* (London: OMF Books, 1965), 5.

Chapter 3: The Hungry, the Fatherless, and the Heart of God

1. A. W. Tozer, *The Pursuit of God* (Harrisburg, PA: Christian Publications, 1948), Kindle edition, chapter 1.

2. Andy Stanley, *How to Be Rich: It's Not What You Have. It's What You Do With What You Have* (Grand Rapids, MI: Zondervan, 2013), Kindle edition, loc. 146.

3. Learn more about Lovelle and her ministry at www.lovellegerthmyers .com.

4. Amy Lively, *How to Love Your Neighbor Without Being Weird* (Minneapolis: Bethany House, 2015), 197.

Chapter 4: Loving People You Don't Want to Love

1. Michele Cushatt, *Undone: A Story of Making Peace With an Unexpected Life* (Grand Rapids, MI: Zondervan, 2015), 40–41.

2. Charles Lee, "5 Ways to Love People Like Jesus Did," ChurchLeaders .com, accessed December 15, 2015, http://www.churchleaders.com/worship /worship-blogs/160221-charles_lee_what_jesus_taught_me_about_human _care.html.

Chapter 5: Why Do You Believe?

1. Brennan Manning, *The Furious Longing of God* (Colorado Springs: David C. Cook, 2009), 117–118.

Chapter 6: Believing Big When You Feel Small

1. Linda Lesniewski, *Women at the Cross: Experiencing the Wonder and Mystery of Christ's Love* (Grand Rapids, MI: Revell, 2005), Kindle edition, loc. 371.

2. Rex Rouis, Twitter tagline, accessed December 16, 2015, https://twitter .com/hopefaithprayer.

Chapter 7: Living a Life of Thank-You

1. Pat Layton, *Life Unstuck*, (Grand Rapids, MI: Revell, 2015), 150.

2. Brad Formsma, *I Like Giving: The Transforming Power of a Generous Life* (Colorado Springs: WaterBrook Multnomah, 2014), Kindle edition, introduction.

Chapter 8: When You Feel Like the Chair Guy

1. Christine Caine, *Unstoppable: Running the Race You Were Born to Win* (Grand Rapids, MI: Zondervan, 2014), Kindle edition, chapter 4.

2. Ibid., 56.

3. Lysa TerKeurst, *The Best Yes: Making Wise Decisions in the Midst of Endless Demands* (Nashville: Nelson Books, 2014), 221–222.

Chapter 9: The Fallacy of a Storm-Free Life

1. Ray Boltz and Lawrence Chewning, "The Anchor Holds," Word Music, 1995.

Chapter 11: Walking Into the Deep

1. Oswald Chambers, "The Purpose of Prayer," accessed December 22, 2015, http://utmost.org/the-purpose-of-prayer/.
2. Ibid.

Chapter 12: Go . . . and Give

1. Abraham Kuyper, quoted in James D. Bratt, ed., *Abraham Kuyper: A Centennial Reader* (Grand Rapids, MI: Eerdmans, 1998), 488.

Suzie (as friends call her) loves nothing more than coming alongside women to gently lead them in a new direction in family, feelings, and faith. Suzie is an author and international speaker with Proverbs 31 Ministries (www.proverbs31.org).

She contributes to *Encouragement for Today*, a daily devotional that reaches 850,000 women around the world. Suzie is a Bible Gateway blogger and shares encouragement through KLRC radio's *Words That Make a Positive Difference*.

She's a wife, mom, and "Gaga" to six babies under the age of five. She believes that being a Gaga is the most fun job she's ever had. When Suzie's not writing or speaking, she's hiking, tending her garden, or rafting down a river.

Connect With Suzie

If you have grown in your faith or God is doing a work in your heart, or you just need someone to pray with you, I'd would love to hear from you.

www.tsuzanneeller.com/contact
www.facebook.com/SuzanneEllerP31
www.twitter.com/suzanneeller
www.pinterest.com/suzieeller
www.instagram.com/suzanneeller
www.periscope.tv/suzanneeller

If *Come With Me* has started you on your journey as the thirteenth disciple, please tell others. I write and speak because it's a privilege and I'm humbled by it. When you spread the word, you partner with me in this, and I'm so thankful.

You can do that by writing a book review on Amazon.com, BarnesandNoble.com, Christianbook.com, or any other online site. You can do that by sharing your book with a friend or passing it along when you've finished reading it. I love to hear about friends who give it to the library, drop it at a local Laundromat, or share it with a ministry library. You can begin a Bible study in your home or share it with your small-group leader. All of these make this girl's heart fill with gratitude, because it's not about the numbers or a book, it's about the people who read it and find Jesus waiting in the pages.

Proverbs 31
MINISTRIES

If you were inspired by *Come With Me* and desire to deepen your own personal relationship with Christ, I encourage you to connect with Proverbs 31 Ministries.

Proverbs 31 Ministries exists to be a trusted friend that will take you by the hand and walk by your side, leading you one step closer to the heart of God through these resources:

- *Encouragement for Today* daily online devotions
- Daily radio program
- Books and resources
- Online Bible studies
- Dynamic speakers with life-changing messages
- Compel Training for those with a heart to write words that move

To learn more about Proverbs 31 Ministries, visit www .proverbs31.org.

More From Suzanne Eller

To learn more about Suzanne, visit tsuzanneeller.com.

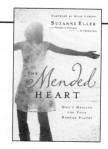

Brokenness happens. When we experience heartache, we often attempt to fix our own brokenness—with disastrous results. If you've tried to heal on your own but keep ending up in the same place, there is good news: Jesus has already completed the work that needs to be done! *The Mended Heart* will encourage you to trust Him, to give and receive grace, and to move ahead even stronger than before.

The Mended Heart

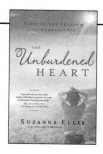

The word *forgive* is not one-dimensional. It does not just mean to "let go and let God." Explore the many facets of forgiveness through Scripture, focusing on the idea of leaving one place to go to another. Discover how, with God's help, you can leave pain to find wholeness, leave regret to find purpose, and leave the past to live fully in the present.

The Unburdened Heart